Decorative Flower Painting

This book is dedicated
to the memory of my husband,
Aubrey "Blackie" Edwards.

Decorative Flower Painting

Ginger Edwards

Sterling Publishing Co., Inc.
New York

Prolific Impressions Production Staff:

Editor in Chief: Mickey Baskett
Copy Editor: Phyllis Mueller
Graphics: Dianne Miller, Karen Turpin
Styling: Kirsten Jones
Photography: Jerry Mucklow
Administration: Jim Baskett

Library of Congress Cataloging-in-Publication Data Available

10 9 8 7 6 5 4 3 2 1

Published by Sterling Publishing Company, Inc.
387 Park Avenue South, New York, N.Y. 10016

Produced by Prolific Impressions, Inc.
160 South Candler St., Decatur, GA 30030

© 2002 by Prolific Impressions, Inc.

Distributed in Canada by Sterling Publishing
c/o Canadian Manda Group, One Atlantic Avenue, Suite 105
Toronto, Ontario, Canada M6K 3E7
Distributed in Great Britain and Europe by Chrysalis Books
64 Brewery Road, London N7 9NT, England
Distributed in Australia by Capricorn Link (Australia) Pty. Ltd.
P.O. Box 704, Winsor, NSW 2756 Australia

The author would like to thank the following companies for supply painting products for creating the projects in this book:

Plaid Enterprises, Inc.
www.plaidonline.com
FolkArt® Acrylic Colors and FolkArt® Artist Pigments.

Bette Byrd Brushes
P.O. Box 2526
Duluth, GA 30096
www.bettebyrdbrushes.com
Artist painting brushes.

About the Artist
GINGER EDWARDS

I have been designing and painting 30 plus years and have not once grown tired of it. Sure, many times I become fatigued, but even when my brushes and paints are set aside for awhile I'm busy planning my next endeavor. In this book, I want to share information that will get you started on your own creative endeavors.

I was raised by parents who loved gardening and flowers. Consequently, flowers have been an enduring favorite subject, a source of pleasure, and a challenge to paint, regardless the medium or surface I choose. In recent years, I've combined my love of junking – collecting discarded furniture and accessory treasures – with painting to create unique pieces. The satisfaction of taking a castoff and turning it into something beautiful and useful is unparalleled.

Long before taking my first art class I wanted to duplicate the beautiful pieces I saw in decorator shops and magazines. Learning how is an ongoing process. Each project presents new opportunities for creativity and learning, whether it's trying a different method of preparation, new color combinations, or finding a useful purpose for a found treasure. Whether I am refurbishing castoffs, updating something I already own, or starting from scratch with an unfinished piece, painting is an absorbing, pleasurable experience.

Ginger Edwards

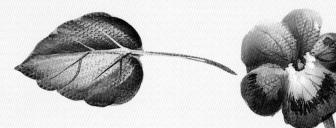

8

Finding, preparing, decorating, and displaying
are all fun parts of the creative process. In this book,
you'll find information about:

• Finding "treasures" to decorate.

• Creating lovely surface backgrounds. (Refinishing is **not** fun, so
I don't do that. Creating lovely backgrounds is fun as well as an
important, integral part of the decoration.

• Enhancing surfaces with decorative painting. Whether you copy my
designs or use them as inspiration for your own, the information
included with the step-by-step worksheets for each flower will be of
invaluable assistance.

• Displaying and using your painted treasures.
Simply painted pieces, when thoughtfully displayed, can have a
profound effect in a room. Using your decorated treasures is infinitely
more satisfying than just looking at them, so
I've suggested various uses for the examples in
this book.

I hope I've sparked your imagination and
desire to begin your treasure hunt. Believe me,
it's great fun! But be warned, it's habit forming!

ginger Edwards

9

SUPPLIES

The supplies needed to create these projects are not elaborate – paints and brushes are the most important. If you are a decorative painter, you may already have many of the supplies you need.

When you have decided on a project, make a list of the supplies needed and gather them together. Assemble them by categories and have them readily available for easy access. Nothing is more frustrating than to be in the middle of a project and discover you are missing an important item.

Keep and store your supplies together once assembled. Do this religiously. This eliminates the time needed to repeat the chore every time you have a new project. It is much more pleasurable to be able to start immediately when the creative urges hit if the basic supplies are at hand and available.

PAINT

Bottle acrylic paints are my paints of choice for decorative painting.
However, many artists prefer tube acrylics. Either can be used to paint the
designs in this book. I have given colors swatches of the paints I have used for
each of the projects so that you can match these colors to the type or brand of
paint you prefer to use for painting.

Acrylic Paints for Decorative Painting

The projects pictured within this book were painted with
bottle acrylic paints that were especially formulated for
decorative painting. Many good brands are available at your
local art and craft store or online where painting supplies
are sold. Be sure to purchase the type of heavily pigmented
paint that is meant for decorative painting.

Acrylic paints are very versatile. Not only are they used to
paint the flower designs, but many of the colors are opaque
and can be used as base paints for surface backgrounds.
When thinned with an acrylic medium or water, they can
be used for shading or tinting a design.

Tube Acrylics

These types of paints are also acceptable to use for
decorative painting and can be purchased at art and craft
shops or on line. Generally, tube acrylics are more
transparent than bottle acrylic paints, which makes them
ideal for tinting and shading but not as desirable for
basecoating. They can be made more opaque for
basecoating various elements of the design with the
addition of white.

PAINTING MEDIUMS

By definition, mediums are liquids with which pigment
is mixed to create an effect. Water is one medium used to
thin waterbase (acrylic) paints to create a desired effect or to
aid in brushing and blending, but it can cause paint to dry
unevenly. Products designed for specific purposes – such as
floating medium, which aids floating for shading and high-

lighting – have properties that aid in accomplishing these
tasks. They dry more evenly than water, allowing greater
open time and greater success. Glazing medium is especially helpful in thinning the painting for antiquing or sponging.

BRUSHES

Buy very good quality brushes and take meticulous care of them. It is one of the best investments you will ever make. Well cared for, good quality brushes last twice as long as cheap ones. Your work will be no better than your brushes, and **it is impossible to achieve good results** if your brushes are not in good shape.

These are the brushes I always have with my supplies:

Rounds – #2, #4, #6, #8

These brushes can be flattened when loaded with a rich mixture of paint and used to fill an area with color, they can be flattened when loaded with a thin mixture of paint to dry-brush high-lights on a surface, and the pointed tips can be used to paint narrow lines.

Liners – 10/0, #1, #2

These brushes are round, with bristles a bit longer than those brushes designated as "rounds." The smallest ones are used to paint final details, such as veins in leaves or petals, while the larger sizes can paint stems or twigs. Larger liners can be flattened when loading with small amounts of paint to dry brush highlights on small objects.

Flats – 1-1/2", 1", #20, #16, #14, #12, #10, #8, #6, #4, #2

These brushes are flat with square corners. The bristles are a bit longer than brushes designated as "brights" or "shaders." The 1-1/2" and 1" sizes are good for applying the topcoat of paint over crackle medium or for varnishing furniture.

Round brushes, *top to bottom*, #6, #5

Liner brushes, *top to bottom*, , #2, #1, 10/0, 10/0

Flat brushes, *top to bottom*, 1-1/2", 1"

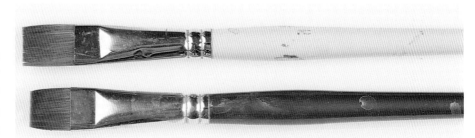

Flat brushes, *top to bottom*, #16 flat, #16 shader or bright

12

Filberts – #8, #6, #4, #2

These brushes are flat but have rounded corners. I use them to stroke flower petals such as daisies. They are also suitable for base painting and blending.

Filbert brushes, *top to bottom,* #12 filbert, #6 filbert, #6 short filbert

Blenders – 1", 3/8", 1/4"

These brushes have soft bristles and are meant to be used dry to give a final blending to paints. They are sometimes called "mops." If you rinse a blender brush with water, you can make certain it is dry by drying it with a hair dryer on low setting before using it again.

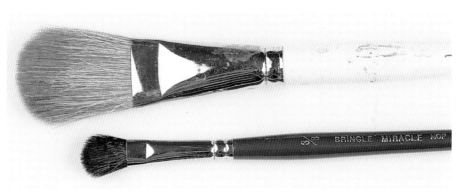

Blender or mop brushes, *top to bottom,* #1 mop (7/8"), 3/8" mop

Filbert Rakes – 1/4"

Depending on brand, they may be called whisks, combs, or wings. These brushes are flat with rounded corners but have fewer bristles than a regular flat brush. They are designed so the bristles separate when sparingly loaded with a mixture of paint and water. I use them to lightly brush highlights on leaves and petals.

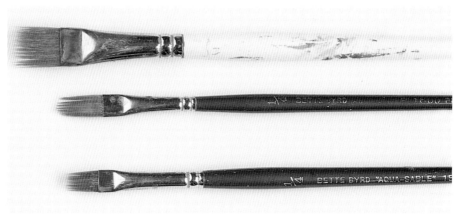

Filbert rakes, *top to bottom,* 1/2" rake (or comb), 1/4" filbert, 1/4" flat whisk

PREPARATION & FINISHING

Pictured left to right: Spackling paste, wood sealer, crackle medium, stain-blocking primer/sealer, glazing medium, matte acrylic sealer spray.

three sides of a square piece of foam about 4" long. They are available in many grits, often with two grits on the same block.

Emery boards are great to have on hand for sanding small areas. Find them in discount stores in the cosmetics section. A **crumpled piece of a brown paper bag** works beautifully to buff your painted furniture prior to decorating.

Tack Cloth is used to wipe away sanding dust. Each can be used multiple times, and should be stored in a plastic bag between uses. They are available at building materials stores in the paint department.

Sanding Materials

Sandpaper is needed to smooth unfinished pieces prior to painting, smooth dry paint between coats, and dull an existing finish so it will accept a new coat of paint. Keep a variety of grits on hand. Numbers on the backs of sheets denote grit; the higher the number, the finer the grit. Sandpaper is available at home improvement centers and hardware stores.

Coarse: Used only under dire circumstances. Coarse sandpaper will cut into paint (or wood) quickly, so be careful. Bad blemishes on wood or glossy enameled surfaces occasionally benefit from light sanding with coarse sandpaper.

Medium: Best all-purpose sandpaper for smoothing wood prior to sealing or basecoating.

Fine and Extra Fine: Good for sanding between coats of paint and for smoothing the prepared project for receiving decoration.

Wet Sandpaper: Is 220 grit and made to be used on a wet surface to produce a mirror smooth finish. The surface is prepared with 3 or more coats of paint, dried thoroughly, then wet with water prior to sanding.

Fingernail Sanding Blocks can be good sanding tools for preparing your furniture. These blocks have sanding grit on

Primers

Primers are paints applied to a surface prior to painting. They are available at home improvement and paint stores. Read the labels to determine if they are compatible with what you plan to apply over them.

Primers for Wood (usually white) are formulated to prevent stains from bleeding through the base paint – they are often referred to as stain-blocking primers or sealers. Priming is an especially important step when painting pieces that previously have been stained and varnished – nothing is more disheartening than having a beautifully painted and decorated object marred from stain bleeding through the finish.

Wood primers come in oil and waterbase formulations as both aerosols and liquids.

Primers for Metal (usually gray or brown in color) are used as a first coat for metal pieces. They come in brush-on liquids or aerosols and dry to a flat finish. Usually, they are oil-based products. I prefer aerosol metal primer.

Sealers

Wood Sealer is designed to be applied to raw wood prior to staining or painting. It fills the grain of the wood so that stain will be absorbed more evenly and protects furniture from humidity as well. It is available at home improvement stores.

You can mix your own sealer with equal parts denatured alcohol and shellac. Store in an airtight container.

Matte Acrylic Sealer is an aerosol finish used to lightly mist prepared furniture for temporary protection. A light coat of matte acrylic sealer applied prior to transferring a pattern and decorating will protect the surface background and make it easier to clean up mistakes. Find it at art supply and crafts stores.

Crackle Mediums

Use **crackle mediums** to create the effect of age – it's quite dramatic. The crackle medium is brushed on a stained or painted surface, allowed to dry (I like to wait 6 to 8 hours – I find I get better results that way), and brushed with a topcoat of paint. Cracks appear in the top coat of paint as it dries.

Crackle mediums can be found at crafts stores, paint stores, and the paint departments of home improvement centers. Follow the manufacturer's instructions for use.

Ink Pens

I use ink pens to add lettering. Ink also can be used to embellish a painted design with accent lines. (For examples, see the cabinet in the Iris section, where I used brown ink, and the painted metal basket in the Violets section, on which white ink was used.) Find these pens where art supplies are sold.

Painter's Masking Tape

This product is manufactured specifically so that the adhesive releases easily, and it comes in several widths. There are varying limits for how long the tape can be left in place so read labels carefully before purchase. Use it to protect areas from receiving paint during base painting. It is invaluable for creating borders. Available at paint and home improvement stores.

Fillers

Spackling paste fills nail holes as well as gouges and cracks. For ease, look for a spackling paste that is ready-mixed and does not shrink. **Water putty** is a powder intended to be mixed with water that can be used to fill holes. It is non-shrinking. Find fillers at paint and home improvement stores.

For Marking, Tracing & Transferring

Use a **soapstone pencil or chalk pencil** for marking placement of borders on prepared surfaces or to sketch designs. Both are water-soluble and can be wiped off easily. They are available at craft and art supply stores.

Tracing paper is used for tracing patterns. The paper is semi-transparent so that the surface is visible through the paper. Find it at your local crafts store.

Transfer paper works like carbon paper to transfer a traced design to a surface. **Water soluble transfer paper** dissolves with moisture and eliminates having to erase pattern lines after painting. Find these products at your local craft store. **Do not** under any circumstances use carbon paper – it will bleed through the paint. Use a **stylus** to lightly trace pattern lines for transferring.

Use an **eraser** to remove visible pattern lines after the design is painted and thoroughly dry. Available at art supply stores. A **soft cloth dampened with mineral spirits** also can be used to remove stubborn pattern lines. Be sure the paint is thoroughly dry before doing this.

Ruler and French Curve

Use a **ruler** to measure and mark placement of borders and patterns. A **French curve** aids placing designs and creating your own designs. They are available at craft and office supply stores.

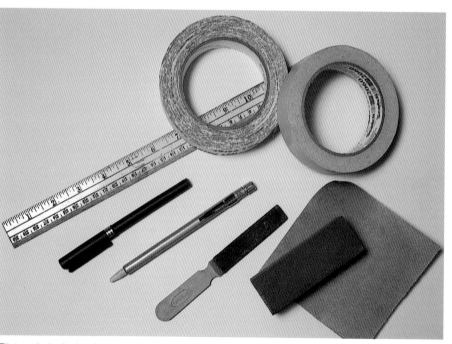

Pictured clockwise from center top: low tack masking tapes, sandpaper, sanding block, emery board, soapstone pencil, ink pen, ruler.

Choosing Surfaces

Begin your quest for items to decorate in your own home or that of a relative or friend. Often, perfectly good pieces of furniture are relegated to the attic or basement (and then forgotten) simply because they are outdated or no longer needed for their intended purpose.

Garage sales, tag sales, thrift stores, and flea markets are wonderful sources for good pieces at little cost. It's true, the early bird gets the worm, so arrive early for the best buys. Make friends with employees at local thrift stores — they might be persuaded to call you when interesting pieces are brought in.

Generally, the finish on a piece has little bearing on whether I purchase it or not, but do carefully inspect pieces you find to make sure they are structurally sound. If you encounter one that isn't, no matter how low the cost or pretty the piece, don't buy it unless you have access to someone who can (and will) make repairs at a reasonable cost.

It's a good idea to locate people who specialize in this type work before beginning your quest for furniture. Call the local senior citizens' centers to ask about retirees working at home. Ask about prices, length of time they usually keep a piece, and names of customers (for references). It's not a bargain if you spend mega bucks to repair something just to make it usable.

Antique shops (but not the ones that specialize in really fine pieces) also are good sources for accent pieces. Expect to pay more — but often you find really neat stuff. It should go without saying that I **do not** devalue fine antiques by altering their appearance or finish with decorative painting.

Craft shows and unfinished furniture stores are sources for unfinished pieces.

Paint Applicators

Palette knife for filling nail holes or blemishes and for mixing paint.

Sponge brushes come in several widths and are good for base painting. White bristle (sometimes called China bristle) brushes are available in several widths and are good for cleaning crevices after sanding as well as for applying stain.

Paint rollers, which come in small sizes with dense foam rollers, are excellent for applying base paint to large flat surfaces such as headboards and tabletops. Available at paint and home improvement stores.

For Special Effects

Assemble an assortment of **natural sponges**. Various effects can be achieved with a sponge according to the size holes and how it is used. Sponges are available in bags of assorted sizes or individually. Sometimes you are lucky and find some that are cut into slices, revealing the holes inside. You can slice a dry sponge with an electric knife or band saw. Sponges are available at crafts or paint stores.

Wedge-shaped sponges designed for applying makeup are great for applying paint evenly to edges of furniture. Find them where cosmetics are sold.

Doilies come in a variety of sizes and styles in both paper and foil. (Foil doilies are stronger and a bit easier to use.) They can be used as stencils to reproduce the effect of a doily on tabletops. Use **spray adhesive** on the back of a paper doily to temporarily adhere it to furniture.

Varnishes

Varnishes are the final protection for your decorated furniture. Functional pieces such as tables and chairs must be protected with a durable finish, such as a clear satin polyurethane finish or waterbase varnish. Decorative objects that are not handled (such as picture frames or plaques) can be protected with a matte acrylic spray.

Pictured clockwise from top: Paper doilies, foam roller, sponge brushes, small square foam sponge, old toothbrush (for spattering), palette knife, sea sponges.

GENERAL INFORMATION

This section includes preparation techniques for creating backgrounds for painted designs on surfaces. I like the look of age, and the techniques I use are ones that work with and enhance the way a piece looked when I found it.

Occasionally, I buy pieces that have many layers of thick paint and aren't suitable for yet another. I pay to have these pieces stripped. Most people who repair furniture will also strip off old paints and finishes. There are many good products available if you want to do the work yourself. Read the cautions carefully before you begin and follow the manufacturer's instructions.

Most times I can prepare a piece of furniture myself without resorting to refinishing.

Finishes

Stained Finish – Traditional Method

This is what I do if the stain is not going to be covered with paint. This is appropriate to use on new, raw wood as well as wood that has been stripped.

PREPARING FOR STAIN

1. Fill nail holes and any blemishes with wood filler or spackling paste. A palette knife is my tool of choice. Let the filler dry.
2. Use medium or fine grit sandpaper to smooth the surface. Sand with the grain of the wood. Wipe away the sanding dust.
3. Brush a light, even coat of sanding sealer over all the surfaces. This fills the pores of the wood so the finish will be absorbed evenly, and it helps prevent warping and cracking. Allow to dry. (The sanding sealer will raise the grain of the wood, causing the surface to feel somewhat rough.)
4. Sand again with fine grade sandpaper, sanding with the grain of the wood.
5. After all surfaces are sanded, wipe with a tack cloth to remove sanding particles. Use a dry brush to clean crevices. You are now ready to stain your project.

STAINING

Most often, I mix my own stain. Artist's oil paint mixed with turpentine or mineral spirits makes a wonderful stain; you can make it as light or dark as you like, and the mixture can be stored for later use. Be sure to work in a well-ventilated area.

1. In a pint jar, mix 1 cup turpentine or mineral spirits and 3 to 4 tablespoons of artist's oil paint (for a brown stain, use Burnt Umber or Raw Umber).
2. Using a 1" or 2" bristle brush, brush this mixture on the surface, working one side at a time. While still wet, wipe off the excess with a clean cloth. Use a clean, dry small brush with soft bristles to smooth stain that might collect in corners or crevices. Allow stain to dry overnight before handling.

Stained Finish – Quick Method

This is the method I use when I want to paint over the stain and sand it to give a worn appearance. This technique is appropriate for new, raw wood or stripped wood.

1. Use a palette knife to fill nail holes or blemishes with wood filler. Let dry.
2. Sand with medium grit, then fine or extra fine grit sandpaper to smooth the surface.
3. Wipe with a tack cloth to remove sanded particles. Clean crevices with a dry brush.
4. Spray evenly with aerosol stain/sealer. While still wet, wipe off the excess with a soft cloth. Use a clean, dry small brush with soft bristles to even out stain that might have collected in corners or crevices. Allow to dry overnight before handling.

Painted Finish with Acrylic Craft Paint

1. Fill nail holes or blemishes with wood filler. Let dry.
2. Sand the project with medium and fine grit sandpaper. Sand with the grain.
3. Wipe with a tack cloth to remove sanding particles. Use a dry brush with soft, clean bristles to clean crevices.
4. With a palette knife, mix 1 part wood sealer with 2 parts acrylic paint.
5. Brush an even coat of the sealer/paint mixture on the surface, using a 1" or 1-1/2" sponge brush. Let dry. (The surface will feel slightly rough, as the sealer/paint mixture raises the grain of the wood.)
6. Sand again with medium or fine grit sandpaper to smooth the surface.
7. Apply a coat of the acrylic paint **without added sealer this time** for a smooth, opaque finish. Let dry before handling.

Painted Finish with Latex Wall Paint

Occasionally, I want to paint a large furniture piece, and using small bottles of acrylic craft paint is neither efficient nor economical. Flat acrylic wall paint is suitable for base painting, and a huge variety of colors is available (You can also select a craft paint color and have it duplicated – just paint a color swatch about 3" square and take it to a paint store. They can match the color by computer and mix it in a larger quantity.)

When base painting with flat acrylic wall paint, sand and seal the project as described in "Preparing for Stain" for the Traditional Method Stained Finish, above. It is important to seal unfinished wood before painting.

Continued on next page

Finishes (cont.)

Aged Finish for Old Wood

Most often I decorate old furniture pieces with existing finishes. I do not want to spend time or money stripping a finish. Here's what I do instead:

1. Clean the piece. If a piece is dirty or if you suspect there is wax buildup, wash it with mild soap and warm water. Wipe dry and allow to thoroughly air dry.

2. Sand the project to smooth and dull the finish so that new paint will adhere properly. Use medium and fine grade sandpapers.

3. Wipe with a tack cloth to remove the sanded particles. Use a clean, dry brush to clean cracks and crevices.

4. Spray or brush on a coat of stain-blocking sealer/primer. (This is white in color and can be used as a base paint as well.) Allow to dry before handling.

5. *Option #1:* If you're using the sealer/primer as a base for decorating, a second application may be necessary for a more opaque coverage. If so, sand the piece lightly, wipe with a tack cloth, and apply a second coat. Allow to dry thoroughly. Sand again lightly before decorating.

   Option #2: If you're using the paint as a sealer to prevent old stain from seeping into a new base paint color, absolutely even, opaque coverage is not necessary. When the first coat of sealer/primer is dry, sand lightly, wipe with a tack cloth, and paint with the color of your choice.

SPECIAL EFFECTS WITH PAINT

Sponging

See Examples 1 and 2 on Worksheet #1.

Sponging can add interest to an otherwise plain area. Sponging is accomplished using a large sea sponge and acrylic paint. Have your surface base painted with a color slightly darker or slightly lighter than the color you wish to sponge. Pour some of your sponging color onto a disposable plate. Dampen the sea sponge. Dip the sea sponge into the paint, then pounce it onto a clean area of your palette or paint to remove some of the excess paint. Then pounce the sponge onto your surface to create the sponged texture. Do not move the sponge around – simply pounce it up and down.

Line Borders

See Example 3 on Worksheet #1.

Use low-tack masking tape to create borders with crisp lines. Measure and rule off the borders you want to create using a straight edge and light pencil marks. Place the tape on either side of the ruled pencil lines. Apply the paint between the tape edges. Allow the paint to dry slightly then remove the paint to reveal crisp straight lines.

Using Doilies As Stencils

See Examples 4 and 5 on Worksheet #1.

Doilies can be used as stencils to create the effect of lace. Lay the doily onto your painted surface. Apply paint onto doily with a sponge in a dabbing technique or by using a paint roller to place paint onto surface.

Crackling

See Examples 6-8 and 11 on Worksheets #2 and #3.

Crackle medium can be used to create a variety of effects that duplicate the look of weather and age on surfaces. There are many brands of crackling medium availble so follow the label directions for the type of medium you are using.

Faux Gilding with Crackle Medium

See Examples 9 and 10 on Worksheet #2.

You can use crackle medium with metallic paint to create a faux gold leafing or gilding – another interesting effect. To duplicate this effect, paint the surface with rusty red or black paint or use a dark stain as a background. Apply crackle medium to the area to be gilded. When it's dry, brush with metallic acrylic paint.

Whitewashing

See Examples 12 and 13 on Worksheet #3.

Colors have a softer appearance when they are brushed with a transparent coat of white or off-white paint, then wiped. This is called whitewashing. The white paint can be thinned with a glazing medium before applied.

Distressing

See Examples 14 and 15 on Worksheet #3.

Sanding can give an aged appearance – the manner in which a piece is sanded makes a difference. Here, paint applied over a stained surface is sanded for two aged looks.

1

2

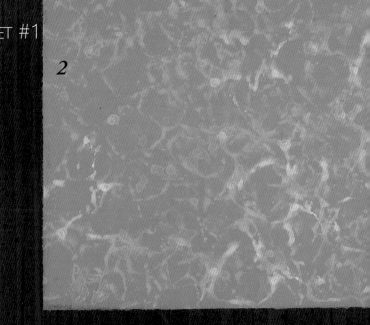

Sponging

Example 1: Light sponging with one color. To create a lighter sponging color, the paint can be thinned with Glazing Medium.

Sponging

Example 2: Heavier sponging, this time with two (related) colors.

3

Example 3: Use tape to protect surrounding areas and define a border; then paint and sponge within the taped area.

Using Doilies As Stencils

Example 4: A doily was positioned on the surface; paint was applied with a foam roller.

Using Doilies As Stencils

Example 5: A softer effect is achieved by using a small piece of natural sponge to lightly pounce paint.

4

5

lightly sponged with metallic gold.

6 Crackling

Example 6: Crackled paint over stain: A black topcoat is applied over crackle medium on a stained surface.

7 Crackling

Example 7: Crackled paint over paint: A white topcoat is applied over crackle medium on a painted surface.

8 Crackling

Example 8: Tiny cracks (sometimes called "eggshell crackle") enhanced with stain: A crackle medium designed to produce tiny cracks is applied over a painted surface. The cracks are rubbed with stain or diluted burnt umber paint to make them more visible

11 Whitewashing

Example 11: A randomly crackled surface can be enhanced by lightly wiping off the whitewash paint in places with a damp cloth to give an aged whitewashed look. Be sure top coat of crackle is dry before whitewashing.

12 Whitewashing

Example 12: Bright yellow paint is much softer looking when whitewashed.

13 Whitewashing

Example 13: Use off-white or beige paint to whitewash darker colors. In this example, beige paint was used, but it appears to be white.

14 Distressing

Example 14: Sanding with long, smooth strokes creates streaks.

15 Distressing

Example 15: Sanding with a light circular motion more closely resembles the age that occurs with use.

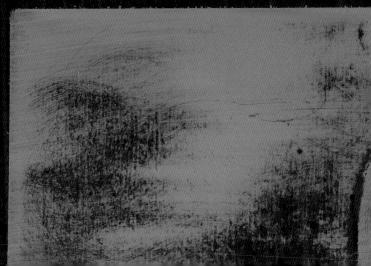

Painting
Terms
&
Techniques

All the designs in this book were painted using a few basic techniques. None is difficult to master. I have given an explanation of each on the following pages.

Ginger
Edwards

Underpaint: To fill a design area with paint. Transfer only the outlines of the design when underpainting. Let the underpainting dry thoroughly, then transfer pattern detail.

Basecoat: To paint the various elements of a design. Usually, I use a middle value color. Occasionally, on large leaves or petals, I use two colors to create the basecoat and blend them while they are wet. That way, I create dimension and maintain a painting guide within a flower or leaf cluster with the very first application of paint. On dark surfaces, my basecoats are most often smooth and opaque. On light surfaces, I sometimes thin the paint with water and a tiny amount of floating medium and stroke it so the background shows through the transparent color. Most often I paint small leaves this way.

Shade: To deepen the color within the design to create dimension. Most often, I apply color with a sideloaded brush. On medium and large petals or leaves, this is most easily accomplished if the surface is slightly moistened with a small amount of water before paint is brushed on. Shading can be applied as many times as necessary to build depth and intensity of color. Let paint dry between layers of color.

Highlight: To lighten and brighten an area. Two or three layers of color are preferable to one heavy one. Generally, I use a filbert rake or liner brush flattened when loading with color to apply highlights. The intensity of highlights is determined by the manner in which they are applied. For subdued highlights, moisten the surface with the barest amount of water prior to stroking on paint. For brighter highlights, brush the paint on a dry surface. *See example on worksheet.*

Sideload: To load a brush so that intense color on one side of the brush gradually fades to nothing on the opposite side. A clean brush moistened with water can be sideloaded with paint; a brush loaded with paint can be sideloaded with a contrasting color.

Stipple: Tapping tips of the brush bristles on the surface to add paint. Highlights on flower centers are often stippled. You can also stipple with a dry brush (round, filbert, or mop) to blend color after it has been applied. Do NOT wash the brush you use to blend paint. If for any reason you must wash the brush, dry the bristles thoroughly before using again. You may dry with a hair dryer on low.

Dry brush: Apply small amounts of paint to a dry surface. Use a rake, whisk, filbert, or round brush (flattened when loading with paint). Load the brush with color. Brush lightly several times on a folded paper towel to remove most of the paint, then lightly stroke the design.

Wet-into-Wet Blending: To apply two colors to an area and blend while wet. Most often this technique is used for large leaves or petals so that contour and definition between petals is established with the first application of paint. Usually, the first layer of paint will appear splotchy and uneven. When the paint has dried and a second layer of paint is applied, the results will be smooth and opaque. *See example on worksheet.*

Tint: Transparent color (thinned paint) applied to certain areas to enhance the design. For example, you can see tints of a contrasting color on the edges of some leaves or petal edges. Tints add variety to a painted design. *See example on worksheet.*

Wash: A layer of transparent color (thinned paint) can be applied over a finished design to alter or enhance the painted (dry) design. More than one color can be used to wash a design to give it sparkle and life. You might choose to wash dull leaves with thinned yellow-green and wash another color on flowers. Dark, rich colors that have little white in them are best for this – how much the paint is thinned determines the intensity of color (see the example with "Tint," above.)

WASH: *Changing the appearance with a wash of color.*

Fig. 1 – White daisies can be altered dramatically with a wash of color. In this example, I used a very thin wine color (Raspberry Wine) to create pink flowers. Any dark color with a little white pigment will work for this technique.

Fig. 2 – Yellow (Raw Sienna) can be washed over flowers and leaves to change their appearance. The color was wiped off the highlight areas of the flower petals while the paint was still wet.

WET-INTO-WET BLENDING: *Apply paint and blending wet-into-wet*

Fig. 1 – How paints look when first applied. Using a flat brush, stroke the darker color first, then sideload the dirty brush with the lighter color. Stroke paint on the petal with the lightest color creating the outside edge. The paints

intermingle even with the first application – the only sharp definition between light and dark colors is where the petals overlap.

Fig. 2 – How paints look when a flat brush is used with short overlapping strokes across the petals (from side to side).

Fig. 3 – A final light blending from the petal tips toward the center of the flower. If the paints streak, it only adds interest. Use a flat or small mop brush for this.

TINT: *One paint color can be thinned with water to create a wide range of values*

The amount of water determines the value. Color range from intense (straight from the bottle) to just a tint (thinned with water for transparent color).

HIGHLIGHT: *The manner in which paint is applied determines the appearance*

Fig. 1 – Paint thinned greatly with water is brushed on a dry surface – good for soft highlights. Use a flat or filbert brush.

Fig. 2 – A highlight brushed on a surface moistened with water. A filbert rake was used.

Fig. 3 – A highlight brushed on a dry surface with a filbert rake.

27

LOADING BRUSHES
Full Loading a Flat Brush

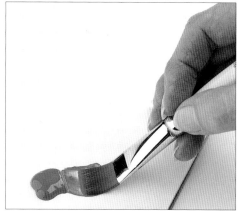

1. Pull paint from a puddle onto the brush. Stroke on palette. Turn over and stroke more.

2. A loaded brush – paint is loaded into bristles – not sitting on top of brush.

Loading Two Colors

1. Fully load brush with paint (here, a medium purple) as you would for full loading.

2. Dip one corner of the brush in the dark value (here, a deep purple).

3. Stroke brush on palette to blend. Turn brush over to blend other side.

4. A stroke with the loaded brush.

Loading Three Colors

1. Load middle value (here, a medium purple) on the brush as you would for full loading.

2. Dip one corner of the brush in the dark value (a deep purple).

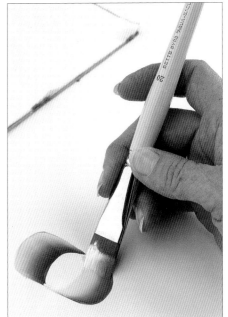

3. Stroke the brush on the palette to blend paint into the bristles.

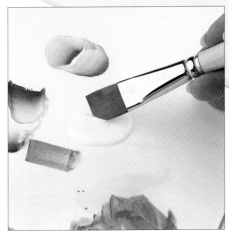

4. Dip the light value (the third color; here, white) on the corner of brush opposite the dark value.

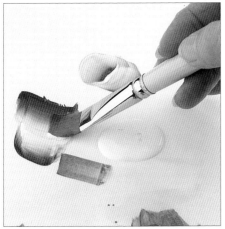

5. Stroke the brush on the palette to blend the colors.

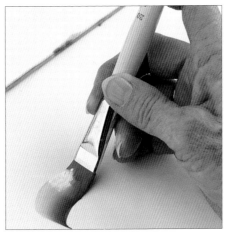

6. Making a curved (convex) stroke with the darker color on the inner edge of the brush.

7. Making a curved (concave) stroke with the darker color on the outer edge of the brush.

29

BRUSH STROKES

Flat Brush Strokes

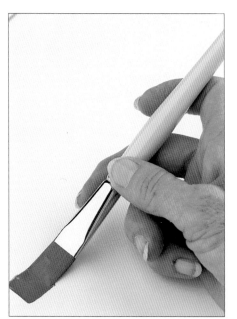

Basic stroke with a flat brush.

Basic stroke with a filbert brush

Making a Stroke with Chisel Edge of Flat Brush

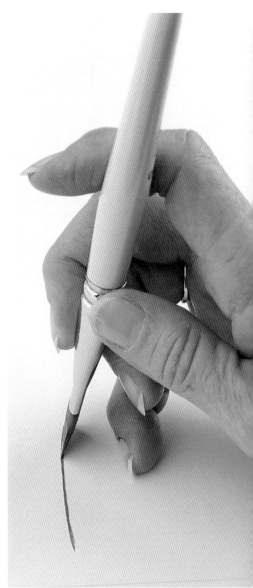

Hold brush straight up and down on the chisel edge (bristles perpendicular to the surface) and pull.

Round Chisel-Edge Stroke with a Filbert Brush

This is the stroke used to make aster petals.

1. Push down with the loaded brush.

2. Lift the brush to end the stroke on the chisel edge.

Round Brush Strokes

This is the stroke used to make daisy petals.

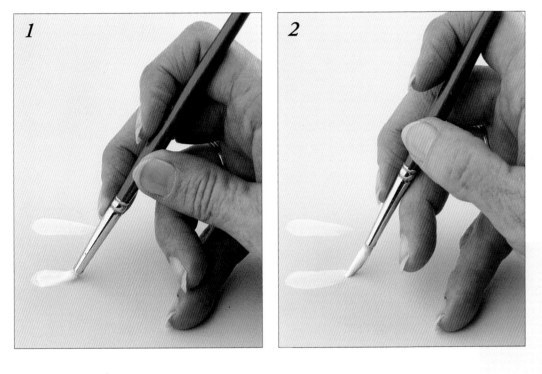

1. Press the loaded brush on the surface.

2. Lift the brush, ending the stroke on the point of the brush.

Liner (or Scroller) Brush Strokes

1. Thin paint with water so it is the consistency of ink. Roll the brush bristles in the inky paint puddle and pull out of the puddle.

2. Make the stroke, holding the brush vertically. The long bristles hold the paint.

BRUSH STROKE TECHNIQUES

Making a Rake Brush with a Round Brush

Flatten the brush as you scrape it around in a paint puddle.

The loaded brush, ready for painting.

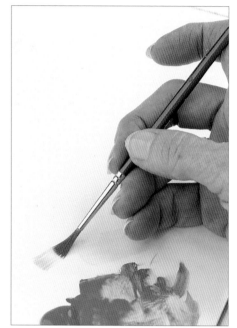

Making a stroke.

Sideloading

Whether the brush is moistened with water or loaded with another paint color, the technique is the same.

1. Moisten the brush with water and blot on a paper towel. Dip one corner of the brush in paint.

2. Stroke the brush lightly several times on your palette to blend and distribute the paint.

3. Turn over the brush and stroke the opposite side of the brush on the palette. Don't stroke too much, or there won't be any paint left on the brush.

Floating Using Floating Medium

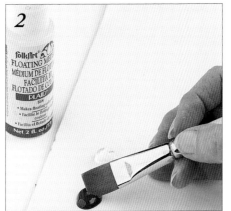

1. Moisten bristles with water and blot on a paper towel. Dip brush in floating medium.

2. Dip one corner of the brush in paint.

3. Stroke on palette to blend and distribute paint.

4. Stroke floated paint on surface. (This photo shows a stroke across the bottom of a cabbage rose.)

Blending Wet into Wet

These photos show wet into wet blending on a leaf.

1. Brush in dark paint in dark areas of leaf. Don't clean the brush.

2. With dirty brush, pick up light color. Fill leaf areas with light color. Wipe (but don't rinse) brush.

3. With dirty brush, stroke to blend the two colors together.

HOW TO PAINT BEAUTIFUL FLOWERS

In the sections that follow, you'll learn how to paint beautiful flowers – asters, daisies, iris, morning glories, pansies, poppies, roses, cabbage roses, sunflowers, and violets – and how to combine them to make painted floral bouquets. Each section tells you the paints and brushes you need and includes step-by-step instructions and a painting worksheet that illustrates techniques. Each section also includes a furniture project (or projects) featuring that flower, with instructions for creating the surface background and finishing.

Displaying & Using Your Treasures

A single, beautifully decorated large chest or cabinet can have great visual impact in a room. Generally, I choose colors for the painting to reflect or blend with those used elsewhere in fabrics and accessories. Very large furniture is cumbersome to prepare and decorate, so I use colors and designs that will blend in when I change decor. Keep in mind a color that is trendy and all the rage now may not be so appealing in a year or two.

Usually, I paint smaller pieces of furniture. One decorated chair in a room may be pretty, but may not make much of a statement. The chair would be displayed to best advantage if elements of the same design were repeated on other pieces (such as a small table or lampshade) and grouped together. Throughout this book, you will see examples of this philosophy. Smaller furniture pieces are much easier to re-do; when you just can't resist that hot new decorator color, use it on a small piece.

ASTERS

Asters are versatile flowers. When used alone, the effect of the various hues is stunning; when grouped with other flowers, the asters' colors enhance and help unify the total design.

Acrylic Paints for Asters

Burnt Sienna	Dioxazine Purple	Lemonade	Lime Yellow	Linen
Night Sky	Periwinkle	Sunflower	Teal Green	Titanium White

How to Paint Asters

Brushes for Painting Asters

Flats – #12, #10, #6   Filberts – #2, #4   Filbert rake – 1/4"   Liner – 10/0
Old worn-out flat brush, #8 (to stipple highlights on flower centers)

Denote main elements of the design:

See Asters Worksheet, Fig. 1.

1. Basecoat all flower centers medium yellow (Sunflower) and leaves beige (Linen). One coat should be sufficient for an opaque coverage. Use flat brushes appropriate to the size area being painted.
2. With a #4 filbert brush, stroke thinned middle value purple (Periwinkle) on flower petals. Let paint dry before continuing.

Begin shading:

See Asters Worksheet, Fig. 2.

1. With a small flat brush sideloaded in reddish brown (Burnt Sienna), shade flower centers. Let paint dry. Deepen shading with an application of darker brown (Burnt Sienna + Burnt Umber). Use the small flat brush sideloaded with paint.
2. Sideload a larger flat brush with dark green (Teal Green). Stroke shading next to center on one side of leaf, then on the base (stem end) of leaf on the opposite side. Let dry.
3. Use the chisel edge of a flat brush or a liner with thinned dark green (Teal Green) to indicate flower stems and any calyxes that might be seen.

Continue shading:

See Asters Worksheet, Fig. 3.

1. Sideload a flat brush with dark green (Teal Green) again. Stroke the paint on the outside edges of the leaf.
2. Sideload the #10 or #12 flat brush and stroke shading across petals next to the centers to give dimension to flowers. Stroke blue-purple (Night Sky) on some, then red-purple (Dioxazine Purple) on others to create variety within the cluster.

Stroke lighter petals:

Stroke a few lighter petals on the flowers in areas that would

catch the most light. Use the #2 or #4 filbert brush with light blue-purple (Titanium White + small amounts of Night Sky) and light red-purple (Titanium White + Dioxazine Purple). See Asters Worksheet, Fig. 4.

Tint leaves:

Sideload a large flat brush with reddish brown (Burnt Sienna) and stroke tints on some of the leaves. Tap the corner of the brush on the leaf to create splotches. See Asters Worksheet, Fig. 4.

Strengthen shading as needed:

See the Asters Worksheet, Fig. 5.

1. On leaves, use dark green that has a brownish tint (Teal Green + a tiny bit of Burnt Umber).
2. On the flowers, repeat the blue (Night Sky) and red purple (Dioxazine Purple) as before.

Highlight:

1. Stroke highlights on leaves. Use a 1/4" filbert rake or a flattened #1 liner for this with light green (Lime Yellow + Lemonade). Stroke the brightest highlights first. The paint remaining in the brush will be sufficient to highlight the dark side of the leaf. See Asters Worksheet, Fig. 5.
2. Highlight flower centers with light yellow (Lemonade). Very lightly touch the worn out flat brush on each center for just the right look. See Asters Worksheet, Fig. 6.
3. Stroke brighter highlights on a few petals in the most prominent flowers. See Asters Worksheet, Fig. 6.

Add finishing touches:

See Asters Worksheet, Fig. 6.

1. If appropriate, stroke some petals over tops of leaves.
2. Shade and highlight a few prominent stems.
3. Paint veins in leaves, using a liner brush. ❑

Asters Worksheet

Fig. 1: Major elements of the design are indicated.

Fig. 2: Shading is begun.

Fig. 3: Edges of leaf are painted; dimension is added to flowers.

Fig. 4: Additional petals are stroked with lighter values of purple hues; leaf is tinted for color interest.

Fig. 5: Shading is added to build depth; leaves are highlighted.

Fig. 6: Design is completed; mottled color is added to background.

Small Accessory Table

This table illustrates how something special can be created from a mass-produced, inexpensive product. The table has a metal base and wooden top. It already had a flat white finish when I purchased it at a home accessory shop in our local mall. While pretty and useful as it was, the hint of a doily and a spray of asters turned it into a personal, one-of-a-kind piece for my home.

It's small enough to fit in many spots, yet large enough to be useful. In a bathroom, it could hold a variety of bath accessories and a jar of potpourri and candle. Placed beside a rocking chair, it's perfect for holding a cup of coffee.

PROJECT SUPPLIES

Project Surface:
Round table

Paints, Mediums & Finishes:
Acrylic paint – soft blue-green
Waterbase varnish
plus acrylic paints for painting asters

Tools & Other Supplies:
Paper doily
Spray adhesive
Small piece of sponge
Large, soft bristle brush
plus brushes for painting asters

PROJECT INSTRUCTIONS

Prepare the Surface Background

This piece was purchased with a flat white finish. Prior to painting the design, I used a paper doily and soft blue-green paint to create a background for the asters and add interest to the tabletop. To duplicate this look, start with a white finish.

1. Spray the back of a paper doily with adhesive. Let dry a minute or two, then position on the tabletop. Be sure that the doily is pressed firmly to the surface.

2. Pour some soft blue-green paint on a palette. Dab a piece of natural sea sponge in the mixture and rub on a palette to distribute paint in the sponge.

3. Tap the paint mixture over the doily on the tabletop.

4. Let paint dry a few minutes, then gently remove the doily. Allow paint to dry completely before handling.

5. Trace and transfer the design.

Paint the Asters

See "How to Paint Asters" and the Asters Worksheet earlier in this section.

Finish the Project

Add final touches to the painting:
Thoughtful placement of color around the design will add interest and draw

Enlarge pattern at 120% or size to fit the project surface.

attention to the focal point. The purple and greens used in the painting are perfect choices for this. See the Asters Worksheet, Fig. 6.

1. Stroke thinned paint onto the surface, then tap lightly with a moist sponge to create a mottled look.

2. Highlight again a few petals on two or three of the most prominent flowers. Stroke a petal or two over a leaf.

Varnish:
Protect the painting with one or two coats of waterbase varnish. ❑

DAISIES

*Whoever coined the phrase "fresh as a daisy" was
onto something. Want to brighten a room?
Daisies are the answer.*

Acrylic Paints for Daisies

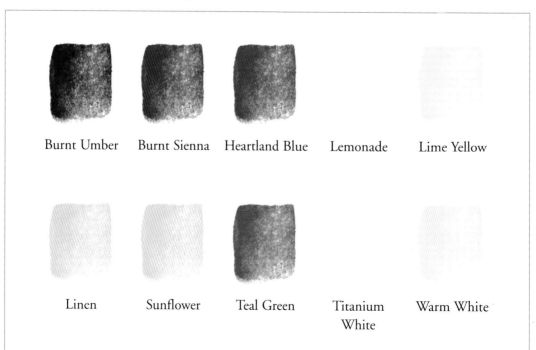

| Burnt Umber | Burnt Sienna | Heartland Blue | Lemonade | Lime Yellow |

| Linen | Sunflower | Teal Green | Titanium White | Warm White |

How to Paint Daisies

Brushes for Painting Daisies

Flats – #12, #10, #6   Liners – #1, 10/0   Filberts – #6, #4   Filbert rake – 1/4"

Establish the various elements of the design:

See the Daisies Worksheet, Fig. 1.

1. Basecoat leaves beige (Linen) and flower centers medium yellow (Sunflower). One coat of paint should be sufficient for an opaque coverage.
2. Stroke petals with thinned blue-green paint (Heartland Blue), using a #6 filbert brush.
3. With dark green (Teal Green) thinned with water to a transparent consistency, establish the buds and flower stems. Use a liner for the stems and a filbert or flat brush for buds. Allow paint to dry.
4. Erase any visible pattern lines.

Begin shading the design:

1. Sideload a large flat brush with dark green (Teal Green). Stroke shading across leaves where petals overlap leaves. Allow paint to dry. See Daisies Worksheet, Fig. 2.
2. Sideload brush again with dark green (Teal Green) and stroke shading on one side of the leaf next to the center vein. Allow paint to dry. See Daisies Worksheet, Fig. 3.
3. Sideload brush again with dark green (Teal Green) and stroke color on outside edges of leaves. See Daisies Worksheet, Fig. 4.
4. Sideload a smaller flat brush with dark green (Teal Green) to shade bottoms of buds and stems where one crosses another or is next to a leaf. See Daisies Worksheet, Fig. 2.
5. Sideload the small brush with reddish brown (Burnt Sienna) and stroke shading on centers. Let dry. See Daisies Worksheet, Fig. 2.
6. Deepen shading on centers with an application of darker brown (Burnt Sienna + Burnt Umber). See Daisies Worksheet, Fig. 3.
7. Sideload a larger (#10 or #12) flat brush with dark brownish green (Teal Green + a small amount of Burnt Umber). Stroke shading on the petals. Shade back petals next to center of flower and front petals on outside edges. Allow paint to dry. See Daisies Worksheet, Fig. 4.
8. Using a #6 or 8 filbert brush stroke, semi-transparent off-white (Warm White) on petals. Let dry. See Daisies Worksheet, Fig. 4.

Refine the painting:

1. Sideload a large flat brush with reddish brown (Burnt Sienna). Stroke tints on the outside edges of some of the leaves. Tap the corner of brush to create splotches. Let dry. See Daisies Worksheet, Fig. 5.
2. Deepen shading as necessary with a brush sideloaded with dark brownish green (Teal Green + a small amount of Burnt Umber).
3. Highlight flower petals. Use a #1 liner brush flattened when loading with paint or a 1/4" filbert rake. Stroke brightest highlights on front petals next to center of flower. Stroke softer highlights on back and side petals half way between the center of flower and tips of petals. See Daisies Worksheet, Fig. 5.
4. Highlight leaves, buds, and stems with very light green (Lime Yellow + Lemonade). Use filbert rakes and liners for this. See Daisies Worksheet, Fig. 5.

Finish the painting:

See Daisies Worksheet, Fig. 6.

1. Use a liner brush and dark green (Teal Green + Burnt Umber) to paint small triangle areas next to the center to separate petals.
2. Highlight the flower centers with light yellow (Lemonade). An old worn-out flat brush is perfect for this. Tap the brush in paint, then very lightly touch the bristles to the surface for just the right amount of highlight.
3. For brightest highlights on petals, use white to which a very tiny speck of yellow has been added (Titanium White + a tiny amount of Lemonade).
4. Paint veins in leaves. Use a light green mixture (Lime Yellow + Lemonade) for center veins and veins painted on dark areas of a leaf. Use dark green (Teal Green) for veins painted on light areas of a leaf. Let dry completely.

Add color in background to enhance the design:

Brush transparent color next to the flowers and leaves with a sideloaded large flat brush. Before paint dries, blot lightly with a damp sponge to create a mottled effect. The blue-green (Heartland Blue) used for the flowers and dark green (Teal Green) used for the leaves are perfect choices. See Worksheet, Fig. 6. ❑

Fig. 1: Elements of the design are indicated with color.

Fig. 2: Shading is begun.

Fig. 3: Shading continues on leaves and flower petals.

Fig. 4: Color is stroked on leaf edges; first highlights are stroked on petals.

Fig. 5: Tints are added to leaves; petals are highlighted.

Fig. 6: The design is completed; mottled color is added to the background.

Cabinet Table

White on white, even painted on a piece prepared to appear worn, is elegant and timeless. In another life, this little wooden table was a tobacco stand. (Another owner had already removed the pipe rack and ash tray that were once attached to the top.)
With an updated finish and decorative painting, I can think of any number of uses for it. In a bathroom, it can hold extra supplies inside and a display of pretty perfumes and oils on top. On a sun porch, a favorite book may be stowed inside for stolen moments relaxing with a cup of tea. And I can't think of a more perfect bedside table for a guest room.

PROJECT SUPPLIES

Project Surface:
Small wooden table with cabinet door

Paints, Mediums & Finishes:
Aerosol (or brush on) stain-blocking primer
Waterbase varnish
plus acrylic paints for painting daisies

Tools & Other Supplies:
Medium and fine grit sandpaper
Small piece of natural sponge
1-1/2" brush, for applying varnish
plus brushes for painting daisies

PROJECT INSTRUCTIONS

Prepare the Surface Background

1. Sand lightly. Wipe away dust.
2. Apply one coat of white stain-blocking primer. Let dry.
3. Sand with medium and fine grit sandpaper to remove some of the paint to reveal the finish underneath.
4. Wipe with a tack cloth.
5. Trace and transfer the design.

Paint the Design

See "How to Paint Daisies" and the Daisies Worksheet earlier in this section.

Finish the Project

After all paint is dry, brush on two or more coats of varnish. ❑

Enlarge pattern at 140% or size to fit project surface.

Cottage Chair with Daisies & Violets

An old kitchen chair with a new, updated look can be used almost anywhere in your home. The color combination on this one is cool and soothing. I decided to decorate the chair with daises. This chair would look wonderful beside a table painted with daisies or one painted with violets. See the "Violets" section showing a charming little drop leaf table that would look great with this chair.

PROJECT SUPPLIES

Project Surface:

Wooden chair

Paints, Mediums & Finishes:

White spray stain-blocking primer

Acrylic paints – Thunder Blue, Dioxazine Purple

Waterbase varnish

plus acrylic paints to paint violets and daisies – see the lists in those sections

Tools & Other Supplies:

Sandpaper – medium and fine grits

Bristle brush, to apply varnish

plus brushes for painting violets and daisies

PROJECT INSTRUCTIONS

Prepare the Surface Background

Since the finish was well worn from use and very clean, no sanding was necessary prior to base painting.

1. Spray the chair with flat white stain-blocking primer. Allow to dry.
2. Sand to smooth the surface and remove some of the primer to reveal the finish underneath.
3. Brush transparent color (paint thinned greatly with water) on some sections of the chair to add interest. I chose a soft blue-violet (Thunder Blue + small amounts of Dioxazine Purple), but soft green or yellow would be equally pretty. Let dry.
4. Trace and transfer the pattern.

Continued on next page

continued from page 49

Paint the Design

Paint the daisies and violets, following the instructions in the "Daisies" and "Violets" sections. See the Daisies Worksheet and the Violet Worksheet for painted examples.

Finish the Project

Protect the painting with two coats of waterbase varnish. ❑

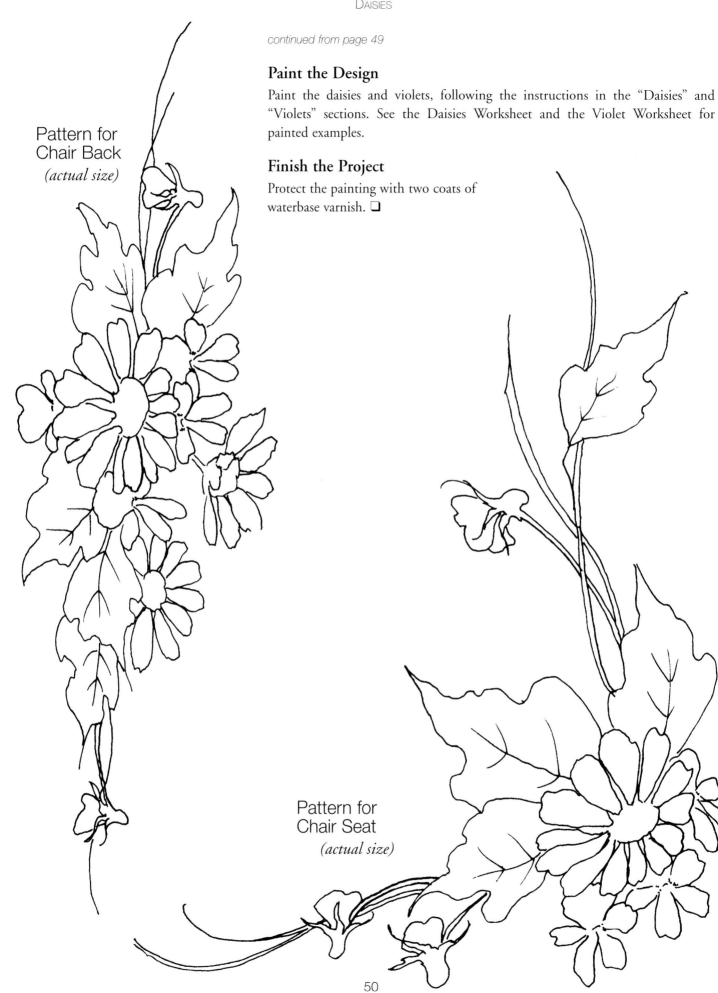

Pattern for
Chair Back
(actual size)

Pattern for
Chair Seat

(actual size)

Wooden Cabinet
Instructions on page 56

Enlarge pattern at 125%
or size to fit project surface.

Dutch Iris

Iris having show... ...ers and s...ord... ...eaves

Iris

IRIS

Iris are tall, handsome flowers with three petals that stand upright (called "standards") and three petals that hang down (called "falls"). Although iris can be found in a range of colors, the blue-purples are my favorites.

Acrylic Paints for Iris

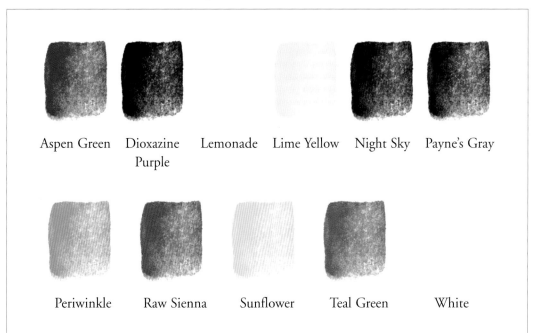

Aspen Green	Dioxazine Purple	Lemonade	Lime Yellow	Night Sky	Payne's Gray

Periwinkle	Raw Sienna	Sunflower	Teal Green	White

Dutch Iris

Iris

having shor... ...ers
and s... orc... ...aves

Iris

How to Paint Iris

Brushes for Painting Iris

Flats – #16, #14, #12, #10   Filbert rake – 1/4"   Small mop
Old, worn-out flat brush (#6 or #8), for stippling stamen

Indicate flowers, stems, and leaves with paint:

Paint petals using two colors, blending while still wet. Paint and blend one petal at a time.

1. Stroke middle value purple (Periwinkle) in darker areas of the petal. Brush white (Titanium White) in remaining areas. Blend while still wet. The paint will appear splotchy and uneven. Let dry. See Iris Worksheet, Fig. 1.
2. Apply a second coat for smooth, opaque coverage. Let paint dry between coats. See Iris Worksheet, Fig. 2.
3. Indicate leaves, calyxes, and stems with thinned light green (Lime Yellow). An opaque coverage is not necessary. See Iris Worksheet, Fig. 1.

Shade leaves, stems, and calyxes to create dimension:

Shade leaves with long smooth strokes of a flat brush pulled the length of the leaf. (If streaks appear, they will only resemble veins seen in this type leaf.)

1. Stroke with thinned medium green (Aspen Green). Let dry. See Iris Worksheet, Fig. 2.
2. Deepen shading using the same brush and darker green (Teal Green + small amounts of Payne's Gray). See Iris Worksheet, Fig. 3.

Shade petals:

Generally, shading on petals is stroked across the petal and then blended, if necessary, by stroking the length of the petal (the direction in which the petal grows). Shading should be applied where petals overlap others and may be stroked on edges as well. Two transparent layers of color is better than one layer opaquely applied. Let paint dry between coats. See the Iris Worksheet, Fig. 3.

1. Sideload a flat brush with middle value purple (Night Sky) and shade petals.
2. Apply a second shading of darker purple (Night Sky + Dioxazine Purple) after the first shading has dried.

Highlight petals and leaves:

See Iris Worksheet, Fig. 4.

1. Highlight leaves, stems, and calyx with light green (Lime Yellow + Lemonade). Dry-brush highlights sparingly on leaves using the 1/4" filbert rake. Flatten a liner when loading with paint to stroke highlights on stems and calyx.
2. Highlight petals with light purple (Titanium White + tiny amounts of Night Sky). Depending on the size area you are highlighting, use either the 1/4" filbert rake or the liner flattened when loading with paint.

Add final details:

See Iris Worksheet, Fig. 4.

1. Paint very light veins in flower petals using a liner brush.
2. Use dark yellow (Raw Sienna + Sunflower) and an old, worn-out brush to stipple stamen on lower flower petals.
3. Stipple highlights of light yellow (Lemonade). ❏

Fig. 1: First coats of paint are applied.

Fig. 2: A second coat of paint is stroked on petals; first shading is stroked on leaf, stem, and calyx.

Fig. 3: Petals are shaded with two transparent coats of paint; shading is deepened on leaves; lettering is inked with a permanent pen.

Fig. 4: Flower and leaf are completed – highlights, veins in petals, and stamen are added; lettering is accented with thinned paint, using a liner brush.

Wooden Cabinet

This small cabinet was purchased new and unfinished. It has wonderful storage space inside, perfect to use for towels in a bath or even as a bedside table. The removable door panel was perfect for decorating. Adding wording gives the feeling of an antique botanical print. The combination of stain and paint on the cabinet gives an old, worn appearance.

PROJECT SUPPLIES

Project Surface:
Wooden cabinet with oval panel

Paints, Mediums & Finishes:
Wood-tone aerosol stain/sealer
Acrylic paints – Soft green (Gray Green), off-white (Warm White)
Floating medium
plus acrylic paints for painting iris

Tools & Other Supplies:
Small piece of natural sponge with an irregular hole pattern
Pen with extra fine point and permanent brown ink
Sandpaper
1" or 1-1/2" sponge brush, for base painting
plus brushes for painting iris

PROJECT INSTRUCTIONS

Prepare the Surface Background

Cabinet:
1. Seal and stain with wood-tone aerosol stain/sealer. Let dry according to manufacturer's instructions.
2. Brush on a coat of soft green (Gray Green) acrylic paint on the sides and door. (Leave the top with just the stained finish.) Let dry.
3. Sand to remove some of paint and reveal the stain underneath.

Panel:
1. Base paint with warm white. Two coats may be necessary for smooth, opaque coverage. Let paint dry and sand lightly between coats.
2. To create the appearance of old parchment, take a damp sponge (wet with water and squeezed dry) and dab a watery mix of brownish-yellow paint (Raw Sienna thinned greatly with water + tiny amounts of Burnt Umber) on the painted surface. Let paint dry thoroughly. (Use a hair dryer on low setting to speed drying.)
3. Spatter with darker brown (Burnt Umber thinned greatly with water). Let dry before handling.
4. Trace and transfer the design. See pattern on page 51.

Paint the Design

See "How to Paint Iris" and the Iris Worksheet earlier in this section.

Finish the Project
1. After all paint is thoroughly dry, draw over the pattern lines of the lettering with the ink pen. Let dry thoroughly. See the Iris Worksheet, Fig. 3.
2. Use thinned brown paint (Burnt Umber) and a liner brush to accent the letters. See Iris Worksheet, Fig. 4. Let dry thoroughly.
3. Erase any visible pattern lines.
4. Protect your furniture with a final varnish. Two coats are preferable. Let dry between coats. ❏

Dutch Iris

Iris

having show[y] [flow]ers and [sw]ord[-shaped l]eaves

MORNING GLORIES

The trailing vines of morning glories make them an easily adaptable subject for a variety of surfaces. The pattern can easily be redrawn to accommodate most any shape. A French curve will aid in creating graceful vines.

Brushes for Painting Morning Glories

Flats – #14, #12, #10, #8   Liners – 10/0, #1   Filbert rake – 1/4"

Acrylic Paints for Morning Glories

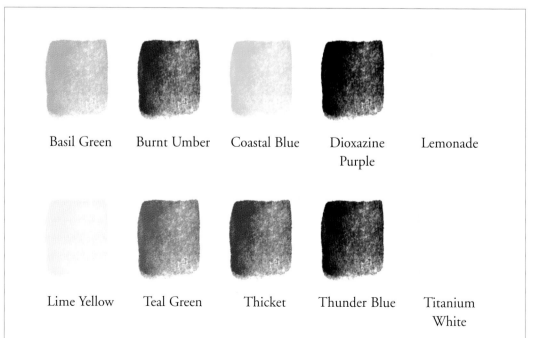

| Basil Green | Burnt Umber | Coastal Blue | Dioxazine Purple | Lemonade |
| Lime Yellow | Teal Green | Thicket | Thunder Blue | Titanium White |

How to Paint Morning Glories

Basecoat flowers:

1. Basecoat the flowers with two colors, blending while still wet, using #10 or #12 flat brushes. First, stroke on white in the light area, then light blue (Coastal Blue + Titanium White) in the space remaining. Blend while still wet. See the Morning Glories Worksheet, Fig. 1.

   • Paint all areas of the flowers having a side view at one time.

   • Paint the flowers with more of the tops showing in three sections. First, base and blend the long throat. Next, base inside the throat and the flower edge further from you and finally base and blend the front portion.

   • When blending the paints, stroke the brush in the direction the flower grows. For example, the long throat would be blended with long strokes from the calyx upwards or from the petal edge downwards. The top of the flower resembles a flared trumpet so paint can be stroked from the edges inward or from the throat outward.

2. Add a second coat of the same colors. See the Morning Glories Worksheet, Fig. 2.

Basecoat leaves, stems, calyxes, and branches:

1. Basecoat leaves, stems (to leaves and flowers), and calyxes a light middle value green (Basil Green). Use #8 or #10 flat brushes on the leaves and #4 or #6 flat brushes for the calyxes. A #1 liner is right for the stems. See the Morning Glories Worksheet, Fig. 2.

2. Use the #1 liner and a thin mixture of brown (Burnt Umber) to paint the branch. Let paint dry.

Lighten the flowers:

Stroke light yellow (Lemonade + Titanium White) inside the throat and next to the calyx, using a large flat brush sideloaded with paint. Let dry. See the Morning Glories Worksheet, Fig. 3.

Shade the various elements of the design:

1. Sideload a flat brush with dark blue (Thunder Blue) to shade the flowers. Shade the trumpet portion of the more open flowers next the flared top. Shade the outside edges, but use only minute amounts of shading on the part in front of the trumpet. See the Morning Glories Worksheet, Fig. 4.

2. Shade the leaves using a #12 or #14 flat brush sideloaded with medium green (Thicket). Refer to Morning Glories Worksheet to see that shading of leaves is done in two

steps – the stem end and center vein area are shaded and allowed to dry (Fig. 3) before the edges are shaded. (Fig. 4).

3. Shade the calyxes with medium green (Thicket), using a #6 or #8 flat brush. See the Worksheet, Fig. 4.

4. Shade stems to leaves and flowers with medium green (Thicket). Allow to dry. See Worksheet, Fig. 5.

5. Use the #1 liner and a darker brown (Burnt Umber with less water) to shade the branches.

Deepen shading on all elements of the design:

See the Morning Glories Worksheet, Fig. 5.

1. Deepen shading on the flowers using blue purple (Thunder Blue + small amounts of Dioxazine Purple).

2. Deepen shading on leaves, calyxes, and stems using a flat brush sideloaded with dark green (Teal Green).

Tint:

See the Morning Glories Worksheet, Fig. 6.

1. Tint some flowers using a flat brush sideloaded with very small amounts of reddish purple (Dioxazine Purple).

2. Tint inside the throats of the flowers with a very tiny amount of brown inside the throats of the flowers, using a sideloaded flat brush.

Highlights:

See the Morning Glories Worksheet, Fig. 6.

1. Use small flat brushes (#6 or #8) and yellowish white (Titanium White + a tiny amount of Lemonade) to stroke highlights on the flowers.

2. Use a filbert rake or flatten a #1 liner when loading with paint to stroke light green (Lime Yellow + small amounts of Lemonade + White) on leaves, stems, and calyxes.

Add final details:

Use a 10/0 liner and paint thinned to the consistency of ink. See the Morning Glories Worksheet, Fig. 6.

1. Stroke the white markings on the flowers with white. Begin at the petal edge and pull towards the center.

2. Paint veins in the leaves. Use light green (Lime Yellow + small amounts of Lemonade + Titanium White) for veins painted on the dark areas of the leaf and dark green (Teal Green) for veins painted on the light areas of the leaf.

3. Paint tendrils, using the liner brush with a green mix (Teal Green + Thicket). ❑

Fig. 1: Flowers are base painted with two colors and blended while wet – with one coat of paint, the color is splotchy and uneven.

Fig. 2: A second application of base paint results in smoother, more opaque coverage; leaves and stems are base painted.

Fig. 3: Yellow tints are added to flowers on throats and next to calyxes (base paint is omitted from one calyx so tint is more visible); the first step of shading on leaves is shown.

Fig. 4: Shading is begun on flowers and calyxes; shading on leaf is deepened.

Fig. 5: Additional shading is added to flowers, leaves, and stems.

Fig. 6: Flowers are completed with the addition of highlights, tints, and linework; highlights are stroked on leaves, calyxes, and stems and allowed to dry; veins are painted on leaves.

Small Square Table
Child's Chair

On this small table, the morning glory design reflects the square corner. The same design was used on the child-size chair, but spread a bit more to reflect the curved seat. The surface preparation makes the two pieces compatible, so they can be displayed together. Any little girl would love this table and chair just her size. Tucked into a corner, it would be a perfect place to display a favorite teddy bear or doll.

PROJECT SUPPLIES

Project Surface:

Square table

Child's chair

Paints, Mediums & Finishes:

Off-white latex paint

Matte acrylic sealer

Waterbase varnish

plus acrylic paints for painting morning glories, bees, and butterflies (see the "Bees & Butterflies" section later in this book)

Tools & Other Supplies:

1-1/2" brush, for applying varnish

Sandpaper

plus brushes for painting morning glories, bees, and butterflies (see the "Bees & Butterflies" section later in this book)

PROJECT INSTRUCTIONS

Prepare the Surface Background

These two projects were purchased with existing finishes. Both were painted blue; however, some white paint was visible on the chair.

For the chair:

1. Sand the chair to expose more white. Wipe away dust.
2. Mist lightly with matte acrylic sealer. Let dry.
3. Trace and transfer the design. I adjusted the pattern for the chair seat, opening it a bit more, then added bees and butterflies.

For the table:

1. Paint with off-white. Let dry.
2. Sand with medium grit sandpaper to remove some of the top coat.
3. Trace and transfer the design or sketch your own. On the table, the pattern was traced in one corner of the top, then reversed and traced on the opposite corner.

Paint the Design

Morning Glories:

See "How to Paint Morning Glories" and the Morning Glories Worksheet earlier in this section.

Bees & Butterflies:

See the "How to Paint Bees & Butterflies" section for step-by-step painting instructions. Let paint dry completely.

Finish the Project

Protect the painted designs with two coats of waterbase varnish. Let dry between coats. ❑

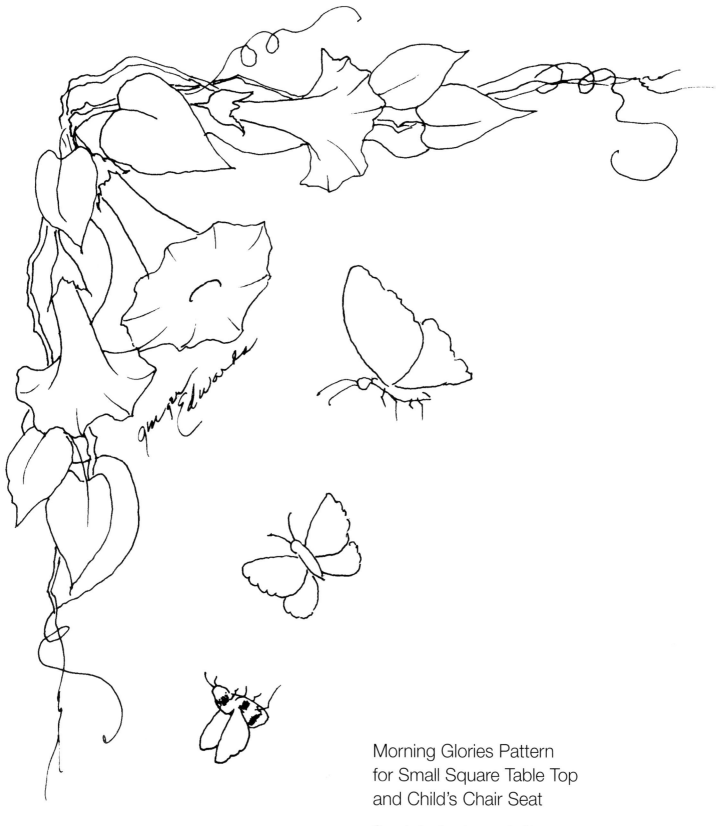

Morning Glories Pattern
for Small Square Table Top
and Child's Chair Seat

*See photos for placement of bees
and butterflies.*

ginger Edwards

PANSIES

There are several varieties of pansy and almost limitless color combinations. I painted mine from live examples, but there are many beautiful photos readily available in magazines and garden catalogs. Jumbo pansies have ruffled petals, while the dwarf varieties have little, if any, ruffling. Viola petals are small and not ruffled.

Acrylic Paints for Pansies

Basil Green

Burnt Umber

Dioxazine Purple

Fuchsia

Lemonade

Lime Yellow

Night Sky

Periwinkle

Sunflower

Teal Green

Thunder Blue

Titanium White

Violet Pansy

Fig. 1: The petals are painted with two colors (a medium value and a very light value) and blended while still wet; leaves, stems, and calyxes are painted a middle value green.

Fig. 2: A second coat of paint applied and blended like the first results in smoother, opaque coverage.

Fig. 3: Petals and buds are tinted; first step of shading on leaves is completed; calyxes and stems are shaded.

Fig. 4: Petals are shaded, adding deeper color and drama; shading on leaves adds the notched appearance on edges.

Fig. 5: More shading separates and defines edges of petals; light yellow is added at throat; stems, leaves, and calyxes are highlighted.

Fig. 6: A liner brush is used to add details.

How to Paint Pansies

Brushes for Painting Panies

Flats – #20, #16, #12, #10, #6   Filbert – #6   Rounded filbert – #6, #4
Liner: 10/0   *Optional:* Small mop

Note: The Pansies Worksheet shows Jumbo Pansies, Violas, and Dwarf Pansies. These instructions tell you how to paint all three. The same techniques and colors used for the petals can also be used on the buds.

Indicate all elements of the design:

Use flat brushes appropriate in size to the area being filled with color. Remember that using brushes that are too small causes more work, and the results are not as good. Filbert brushes are good for painting smaller petals or leaves.

1. Basecoat all leaves, calyxes, and stems with light medium green (Basil Green). See the Pansies Worksheet, Fig. 1, of all three flowers.
2. Basecoat all petals of jumbo and dwarf pansies and the four petals (two side and two top) of the violas, using a wet-into-wet method. Working on one petal at time, stroke white (Titanium White) on the petal in lighter areas, then small amounts of lavender (Periwinkle) in darker areas. Blend while still wet. Complete one petal before moving to the next. Basecoat the lower petal of the viola with white. Paint will appear splotchy. See the Pansies Worksheet, Fig. 1, of all three flowers. Let dry.
3. Apply second basecoats to flowers, leaves, and stems, just as you did the first, using the same colors for a smooth, opaque coverage. See Jumbo Pansies, Fig. 2. Let paint dry.
4. Erase any visible pattern lines since the design is now established.

Shade and tint:

Use sideloaded flat brushes in appropriate sizes.

1. Sideload a flat brush with tiny amounts of fuchsia (Fuchsia). Tint petals of the jumbo pansies (see Jumbo Pansies, Fig. 3) and lower petal of the viola (see Violas, Fig. 3). *Note: You can choose to finish a pansy at this stage. See Jumbo Pansies, Fig. 7 for an example.*
2. Shade petals of jumbo pansies (see Jumbo Pansies, Fig. 4) and dwarf pansies (see Dwarf Pansies, Fig. 2) and upper four viola petals (see Violas, Fig. 2) with dark blue purple (Night Sky).

3. Sideload a large flat brush with dark green (Teal Green). Position brush on one half of the leaf, with the paint side of the brush touching the center vein area next to the stem and stroke shading in the center of the leaf. With the paint remaining in the brush, shade the opposite side of the leaf at the base. See Jumbo Pansies, Fig. 3.
4. Sideload a small flat brush with dark green (Teal Green) to shade tops of calyxes and stems. See Jumbo Pansies, Fig. 3. Let paint dry.
5. Sideload the large brush with dark green (Teal Green) and stroke color on outside edges of the leaf. See Jumbo Pansies, Fig. 4.

Strengthen shading as necessary:

Use sideloaded flat brushes.

1. Strengthen shading on the jumbo pansy with light purple (Violet Pansy). Let dry. See Jumbo Pansies, Fig. 4.
2. Deepen the shading with light purple darkened with dark reddish purple (Violet Pansy + Dioxazine Purple). See Jumbo Pansies, Fig. 5.
3. Strengthen shading on dwarf pansies with dark blue purple (Night Sky).
4. It is not necessary to strengthen shading on the viola petals; tint the petals with small amounts of fuchsia (Fuchsia) if you wish. See Violas, Fig. 4.
5. Deepen shading on leaves if necessary using a large flat brush sideloaded with dark green that has small amounts of brown added to it (Teal Green + small amounts Burnt Umber).

Highlight:

1. Sideload a flat brush (use a #14 or #20 on jumbo pansies and a #10 or #12 on smaller ones) with light yellow (Lemonade + small amounts of Titanium White) to stroke yellow on the lower petals. Position the brush so the paint side of the brush is at the center of the flower. See Jumbo Pansies, Fig. 5 and Dwarf Pansies, Fig. 3.

Continued on page 71

VIOLAS & DWARF PANSIES WORKSHEET

VIOLAS:

Fig. 1: Petals are basecoated; a second coat may be necessary for smooth opaque coverage – let dry between coats.

Fig. 2: Shading is applied to upper four petals; a yellow tint is stroked on the lower petal.

Fig. 3: Petals are tinted with small amounts of transparent color.

DWARF PANSIES:

Fig. 4: Details are added with a liner brush to complete the flower.

Fig. 1: Petals are base painted individually to maintain separation; A second application may be required for smooth, opaque coverage.

Fig. 2: Shading is stroked with a sideloaded flat brush to further define separation.

Fig. 3: Lower petal is stroked with yellow; other petals are highlighted with colors slightly lighter than base colors.

Fig. 4: Flower is finished by adding dot of green in center of throat, veins, darker yellow marking on throat, and pollen on side petals.

Fig. 5 – An Option: Markings are added to create variety

continued from page 69

2. Very little highlighting is required on the petals – use very small amounts of white + a bit of lavender (Periwinkle) if you wish. A liner brush that has been flattened as you load it will work nicely.

3. Highlight leaves, calyxes, and stems with light green (Lime Yellow + small amounts of Lemonade). A filbert rake or flattened liner is a good brush. Stroke the brightest highlights with a freshly loaded brush; stroke softer highlights after most of the paint has been used. See Jumbo Pansies, Fig. 5.

Finish the painting:

1. Use the liner with paint thinned to the consistency of ink to paint veins in flower petals. Use paint corresponding to the color of the petal. Prominent markings on the "face" should be bolder. Use dark blue purple (Night Sky) and dark reddish purple (Night Sky + Dioxazine Purple) for this. See Jumbo Pansies, Figs. 6 and 8 and Dwarf Pansies, Fig. 4.

2. Add the small dot in the center of throat with light medium green (Basil Green). See Jumbo Pansies, Fig. 6, Violas, Fig. 4, and Dwarf Pansies, Fig. 4.

3. Stroke medium yellow (Sunflower) on the very top next to the throat of the lower petal. See Jumbo Pansies, Fig. 6, Violas, Fig. 4, and Dwarf Pansies, Fig. 4.

4. With the liner, tap small amounts of light yellow (Lemonade) to indicate pollen on each side petal. See Jumbo Pansies, Fig. 6, Violas, Fig. 4, and Dwarf Pansies, Fig. 4.

5. Add additional shading to some pansies to create variety. See Jumbo Pansies, Fig. 8, where darker blue violet shading was added to the petals and Dwarf Pansies, Fig. 5, where a row of thin lines were placed side by side. (This shading would be appropriate to add to jumbo pansies as well.)

Pictured above: Pansy Table with Shelf. Instructions follow on next page.

6. Paint veins in the leaves using the liner brush. Paint the center vein and any veins appearing on dark areas of the leaf with light green (Lime Yellow + Lemonade). Paint veins appearing on light areas of the leaf with dark green (Teal Green). See Jumbo Pansies, Fig. 6. ❏

Headboard & Table with Shelf

The bed and table you see cost a total of $5 at tag sales. With little effort, I've created a useful ensemble from pieces most likely headed for the dump. The complementary colors (yellow and purple) and a design that includes several varieties of pansies made this a fun project. This would be beautiful in a young lady's room or a special guest room.

PROJECT SUPPLIES

Project Surfaces:

Bed with headboard

Rectangular table with turned legs and shelf

Paints, Mediums, Finishes:

White latex paint

Butter yellow latex or acrylic paint

Floating medium

Crackle medium

Satin waterbase varnish

Matte acrylic sealer spray

plus acrylic paints for painting pansies

Tools & Other Supplies:

Sandpaper – Medium and fine grits

Rectangular paper doily (for table)

Foam paint roller

Spray adhesive

1-1/2" or 2" sponge brush, for applying top coat of paint

1" white bristle brush

1-1/2" flat brush, for applying top coat and final finish

plus brushes for painting pansies

PROJECT INSTRUCTIONS

Base paint:

Base paint the tabletop white. Base paint all other areas with soft butter yellow. Two coats may be necessary for a smooth opaque coverage. A sponge roller makes this a quick task. Let paint dry and sand lightly between coats.

Crackle:

1. Use the white bristle brush to apply an overall coat of crackle medium on the table legs and apron. Brush crackle medium on the headboard randomly, avoiding the areas you will be decorating. Let dry several hours or overnight.
2. On the headboard, brush on a coat of white paint thinned with very small amounts of water using the 1-1/2" flat brush. Work quickly and avoid repeated brushing in one area. Cracks will form as the paint dries.
3. Brush on a coat of the same mixture on the table apron and legs. Let dry.
4. On the headboard, after cracking has occurred and the paint is dry but not cured, use a soft damp cloth to wipe off some white paint in areas where there is no cracking. (If you wipe where the cracks are, it will soften the crackle medium to the point where it will come off. This can be a good thing if you got carried away and have too many cracks.) I did not wipe any of the white paint off the table apron and legs.

Create the doily effect on the tabletop:

1. Spray the back of the paper doily with adhesive and position it on the surface of the table.

Pansy Patterns for Table with Shelf

Use photo as a guide for placement .

Headboard Pattern

See page 126.

2. Use the roller to apply the yellow base paint color over all the top. Allow to dry a minute, then remove the doily. Let paint dry completely before handling.

3. Check to see if there is any adhesive residue on the tabletop. If there is, remove it with a soft cloth dampened with turpentine or mineral spirits.

Seal:

1. Mist all surfaces of the projects with matte acrylic sealer. Let dry.

2. Transfer the design, or lightly sketch your own. On the tabletop, I randomly scattered flowers traced from the main design.

Paint the Design

See "How to Paint Pansies" in this section.

Finish the Project

When the painting is dry, protect the project with two or more coats of waterbase varnish. ❑

POPPIES

The showy flowers of poppies appear for only a short time – a week or two in the late spring or early summer. The flowers can be red, pink, orange, salmon, or white.

Brushes for Painting Poppies

Flats – #12, #10, #8, #6   Filbert – #6   Liners – #1, 10/0   Filbert rake – 1/4", 1/8"

Acrylic Paints for Poppies

Aspen Green	Burnt Sienna	Burnt Umber	Lemonade	Lime Yellow

Linen	Poppy Red	Raspberry Wine	Red Light	Teal Green

How to Paint Poppies

Establish all elements of the design:

See Poppies Worksheet, Fig. 1.

1. Basecoat petals. Use flat brushes appropriate to the size petal being painted. Finish blending each petal before moving to the next. Brush small amounts of medium red (Poppy Red) in darker areas of the petal. Fill remaining areas with beige (Linen). Wipe the brush and blend while paints are still wet.

2. A second coat of paint may be necessary for a smooth opaque coverage. Let paint dry and apply paints a second time.

3. Brush light green (Lime Yellow) in light areas of the leaf and medium green (Aspen Green) in darker areas. Wipe the brush and blend while still wet. A filbert brush is good for this.

4. Use a smaller flat brush to fill centers with light green (Lime Yellow). While still wet, stroke medium green (Aspen Green) across bottom.

5. Paint stems and buds light green (Lime Yellow).

Begin shading and highlighting:

Use various size flat brushes according to the size of the area being painted. Shading is applied with strokes pulled across the petal and highlights are stroked on the length of the petal. If paints streak slightly, it will only duplicate the streaks seen in real flowers.

1. Sideload a large flat brush sparingly with a dark red mixture (Raspberry Wine + Red Light) thinned with small amounts of water + floating medium. Stroke shading next the center on side and back petals and on outer edges of front petals. See Poppies Worksheet, Fig. 2.

2. While paint is still wet, stroke small amounts of beige (Linen) highlights.

3. Sideload a flat brush with dark green (Teal Green) to shade one side of the leaf next to the center and outside edges. See Poppies Worksheet, Fig. 3. Shade bud with the same color.

4. Shade stems with dark green (Teal Green). Sideload a flat brush and stroke color across the stem where it would be under a leaf or flower petal. If blending is necessary, stroke color the length of the stem. See Poppies Worksheet, Fig. 3.

5. With a flat brush sideloaded with paint, strengthen shading next to center vein on one side of leaf. See Worksheet, Fig. 5.

Tint:

1. Sideload a large flat brush with brownish red (Raspberry Wine + Burnt Sienna) to tint some leaves with color. Position the brush so that the paint side touches the edge of the leaf to stroke color. Tap the corner of the brush on the leaf to add splotches. See the Poppies Worksheet, Fig. 5.

2. Sideload the large flat brush sparingly with thinned medium red (Red Light) and stroke this color on the front leaf where it folds out from the center of the flower. See Worksheet, Fig. 5.

Highlights:

It may not be necessary to add more paint since the painting was begun with very light colors and enough may still be visible to create the highlights. Use these mixtures if additional highlights are desired. See Poppies Worksheet, Fig. 5.

1. Dry brush highlights on leaves and buds with light green (Lime Yellow + Lemonade) using a 1/4" filbert rake or a liner that was flattened when loading with paint.

2. Brush highlights on petals with pale yellow (Lemonade + small amounts of Linen). Depending on your base color, you may choose to add a bit of white (Titanium White) to the highlight mixture. (Because my tabletop was an antique ivory color, I did not use a lighter highlight.)

3. Sideload a flat brush with tiny amounts of Poppy Red and stroke color on the front petal where it folds outward from the center. See Worksheet, Fig. 5.

Add details to finish the painting:

1. Use the #1 liner brush to add light yellow (Lemonade) strokes of paint to the center. Let dry. See Worksheet, Fig. 4.

2. Mix a dark, blackish color (Teal Green + Raspberry Wine in equal amounts) and use the liner brush to paint stamen. See Worksheet, Fig. 5.

3. Tap the brush with the same paint mixture on the surface to create splotches among the stamen. See Worksheet, Fig. 6.

4. Tap lighter splotches (Linen + small amounts of the dark mixture). See Worksheet, Fig. 6.

5. Paint stems and veins using a 10/0 liner with thinned dark green (Teal Green).

6. To paint the prickles on the stems and buds, flatten a 10/0 liner brush when loading with thinned dark green (Teal Green). Use just the tips of the bristles to paint the prickles. You can also use a 1/8" filbert rake. Let paint dry. See Worksheet, Fig. 5.

7. Add a few lighter prickles using the same brush and method of loading with light green (Lime Yellow + Lemonade). See Worksheet, Fig. 6. ❑

Fig. 1: The various elements of the design are base painted using a wet-into-wet technique that defines petals and contours.

Fig. 2: The side and black petals are shaded.

Fig. 3: Shading is added to the front petal, leaf, and stem.

Fig. 4: Details are added to flower center; shading is completed on outside edge of leaf.

Fig. 5: Highlights are brushed on flower petals; stamen are painted; shading is strengthened on one side of leaf; tints are added to leaves; prickles are painted on stem.

Fig. 6: The flower is finished – splotches are added to the center; veins are added to leaf; light prickles are added to stem.

Enamel-Topped Table

Only a true enthusiast of the hunt would have given this old enamel-topped table a second look. The gaudy blue paint on the legs coupled with the rusty spots on top certainly didn't beckon me — at first. It was one of those pieces I got to thinking about later, and I decided it did have possibilities. (Usually, if I can figure out a use for something, I can purchase it with few guilt pangs, especially if the price is right.)

I decided it would be a perfect work table since the rollers on the legs would make moving it easy — I could use it in my studio even if I never decorated it. When I went back to rescue it from the junk store, it was gone!

Then, of course, I began to imagine all sorts of wonderful things I could have done with it. (The one that got away always haunts your thoughts.) By this time, I'd decided it would make the perfect table for a country kitchen or patio. Imagine my surprise when I received it as a Mother's Day gift! I plan to use it in the kitchen as an island/work table. To ensure that acrylic paint would adhere properly, I underpainted the poppies with a stain blocking primer made for slick surfaces. The primer accepts acrylic paint, so it serves as a bonding agent for the acrylic decoration.

My table came with the blue checks on top. You could duplicate the look with a checkerboard stencil and blue paint.

The enamel-topped table before decorating. (The blue checks were part of the original tabletop.) The small square table pictured is one of the projects in the Morning Glories section.

PROJECT SUPPLIES

Project Surface:
Enamel-topped kitchen table

Paints, Mediums & Finishes:
Ivory paint
Bright blue latex paint
Brush-on primer, the kind that "sticks to shiny surfaces"
Satin varnish, for a final protective finish
plus acrylic paints for painting poppies

Tools & Other Supplies:
Sandpaper, medium and fine grits
1-1/2" brush, for applying varnish
plus brushes for painting poppies

Continued on page 80

Ginger
Edwards

PROJECT INSTRUCTIONS

Prepare the Surface

My table came with bright blue legs and apron. I wanted some of the blue color to be visible to coordinate with the checks and the rim on the tabletop, but I wanted to subdue it.

1. Brush on a coat of ivory paint on the legs and apron. Let dry.
2. Sand to remove some of the topcoat.
3. Trace the pattern and transfer the outlines (no details).
4. Carefully underpaint the design with one coat of primer. Let dry thoroughly.
5. Transfer pattern details.

Paint the Design

1. Paint the checks with bright blue.
2. Paint the poppies, following the instructions earlier in this section. See the Poppies Worksheet.

Finish the Project

Brush on a protective finish of satin varnish over all the table, including the top.
❑

Pattern for Table
(actual size)

Connect patterns at dotted lines to complete.

ROSES

Roses are called the "queen of flowers." Painting beautiful roses has been an ongoing learning experience for me – one I never tire of. It is challenging but well worth the time spent to perfect the techniques involved.

Brushes for Painting Roses

Flats – #20, #16, #14, #12, #10, #8, #6
Liners – #1, 10/0   Filberts – #6, #8   Filbert rake – 1/4"   Small mop

Acrylic Paints for Roses

| Burnt Sienna | Burnt Umber | Gray Green | Lemonade | Linen |
| Raw Sienna | Sunflower | Teal Green | Titanium White | Yellow Ochre |

Roses Worksheet

Steps 1 through 6 show how the rose is constructed with just strokes of a brush. (I always construct a rose in middle value tones.) Do not worry about shading and highlights at this point. As long as you can see the various petals, even faintly, you are doing fine. Study the illustrations and read the instructions before you begin.

Roses:

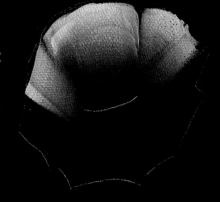

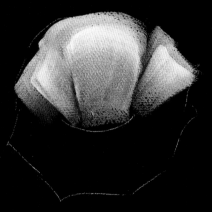

Fig. 1: Petals are transferred; three back petals are stroked. There's no paint in the center of the rose.

Fig. 2: A second layer of petals is stroked slightly inside the first and a bit smaller. There is paint in the center of the flower now as a result of blending the petals lightly.

Fig. 3: The two lower side petals are stroked.

Fig. 4: The lowest petals are indicated.

Fig. 5: The petal at front center is stroked.

Fig. 6: Areas are filled and coverage is strengthened.

ROSES WORKSHEET

ROSES:

Fig. 7: Additional color is stroked to shade and separate the petals. Notice how the center appears deeper and the petal edges brighter when the darker color is added.

Fig. 8: Petal edges are lightened and brightened by sparingly brushing highlights.

ROSEBUDS, HIPS, STEMS & LEAVES

Fig. 9: Final details are added to the flower.

Fig. 10: Leaves, buds, stems, and hips are base painted and shaded.

Fig. 11: Edges of leaves are indicated; a tint is stroked on the bud; dried stamen on rosehip is painted.

Fig. 12: Calyx is stroked on rose hip; splotches are added to stamen; highlights are stroked on leaves; veins are added to bud; thorns are added to stems; stems are highlighted.

Fig. 13: The painting is complete – calyx on hip is shaded and highlighted; highlights are tapped on stamen; stems to leaves and veins on leaves are added.

How to Paint Roses

I have shown each step in detail so you can see the roses are not pretty until the final brush stroke is made. It is all too easy to become discouraged when, with just a little more effort, you will have pleasing results. Allowing the paint to dry between some of the steps will relieve any stress you may feel and give you time to "think it through."

First study the Roses Worksheet. Remember roses won't look good until they are finished, and don't get discouraged. The Roses Worksheet and the following instructions refer to painting a yellow rose; the photos show a pink rose. Whatever the color, the technique is the same.

Basecoat the leaves, hips, and stems:

See Roses Worksheet, Fig. 10. One coat of paint should be sufficient for an opaque coverage. Use small flat brushes (#6, #8, #10 or a #6 filbert).

1. Basecoat leaves and buds with soft green (Gray Green).
2. Basecoat hips and stems with beige (Linen). Let dry.

Paint the rose petals:

*Transfer only the outer edges and a line that represents the stroke directly in front of the center. **Do not** transfer any petals inside the flower.*

1. Establish the rose using a light, middle value yellow (Sunflower) sideloaded with white. Use flat brushes (#20 or #24) appropriate to the area being painted. Place the side of the brush with the lightest color paint on the petal edge. Start on the chisel edge (**photo 1**) and pull to make a pivot stroke (**photo 2**) to paint the back left petal. Make a curved center back stroke next (**photo 3**, then make the right back stroke. If necessary, wipe brush

and blend. (This won't be necessary if brush is loaded properly.) See the Roses Worksheet, Fig. 1.

2. Reload the brush in the same manner. Stroke a second layer of petals slightly inside the first and a bit smaller. Do not leave much space between the top edges of the two rows of petals. Wipe paint from the brush and blend lightly. See Roses Worksheet, Fig. 2.
3. Using the same brush with the same colors, stroke the two lower side petals. Stroke the outermost petal on each side. Reload the brush and add strokes inside the first ones (just as you did for the back petals). See the Roses Worksheet, Fig. 3.
4. Indicate the lowest petals – usually two (or at most three) strokes will suffice. Use the same large flat brush loaded with the same colors. The strokes may be blended, if necessary. If some paint moves into the area underneath the front center petals, that is fine. See the Worksheet, Fig. 4.
5. Use a smaller flat brush (#12 or #14) loaded with the same colors to stroke the petal directly in front of the center. See the Roses Worksheet, Fig. 5. Allow paint to dry.
6. Add petals to fill the area in front of the center. Make thin strokes, starting on the chisel edge (**photo 4**). Press to thicken the stroke (**photo 5**) and end on the chisel edge (**photo 6**). Brush small amounts of paint sparingly to fill areas where there is none or the coverage is thin. See the Worksheet, Fig. 6. Use flat brushes appropriate to the size of the area; for instance, if more paint is needed on the inside back petals, use a #20 or #24. If filling an area underneath the center front petal, use a #10, #12, or #14. The rose is still not finished, but certainly you can tell it's a rose.

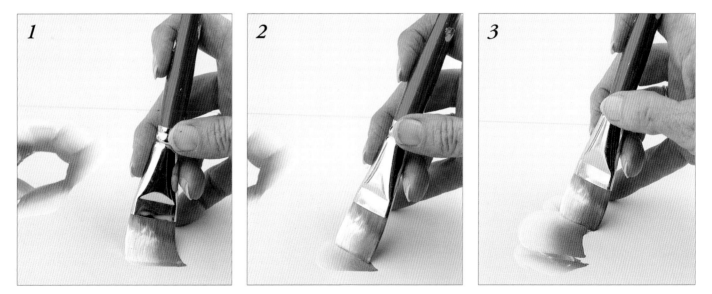

Further define petals:

1. Stroke additional color to shade and further separate the petals, adding color next to a petal edge or in the center of the rose. Use middle value yellow (Yellow Ochre + small amounts of Raw Sienna) sideloaded on flat brushes appropriate to the size of the area being painted. Wipe paint from the brush before blending. See Rose Worksheet, Fig. 7.
   • Small mop brushes aid blending.
   • If the paint does not blend easily, try moistening the surface with small amounts of water + a floating medium before stroking on paint.
   • Apply shading as many times as necessary to create the effect you want. Let dry between applications of paint. Let paint dry before moving to next step.
2. Lighten and brighten petal edges by sparingly brushing highlights. Use flat brushes appropriate to the area. Moisten brush with water + small amounts of floating medium and blot on a folded paper towel. Sideload with light yellow (Titanium White + Lemonade). Stroke highlights on the most prominent petals. See Worksheet, Fig. 8.

Add details to rose:

See the Rose Worksheet, Fig. 9.

1. Stipple dark brown (Burnt Umber + Burnt Sienna) to indicate centers. Use an old, worn-out brush for this.
2. Paint stamen using a liner and the same mixture thinned with a bit of water.
3. Tap tips of the bristles to add splotches among the stamen. Let dry.
4. Add additional splotches of dark (Yellow Ochre) and light yellow (Lemonade).

5. Deepen shading as necessary in triangular areas created where petals overlap. Use a small flat brush (#10) sideloaded with dark yellow (Raw Sienna + small amounts of Burnt Sienna).

Finish the leaves and bud:

1. Sideload a #8 or #10 flat brush with dark green (Teal Green). Stroke shading on the bud, hip, and some leaves. See the Rose Worksheet, Fig. 10.
2. Shade other leaves with reddish brown (Burnt Sienna + small amounts of Burnt Umber). Stroke shading next to center of leaf on one side, then at the base (stem end) on opposite side. See the Rose Worksheet, Fig. 10. Let dry.
3. Indicate edges of leaves using a #10 or 12 flat brush sideloaded with paint – use the same colors used for center veins on the various leaves. On some green leaves, paint a brown edge. See the Rose Worksheet, Fig. 11.
4. To add splotches to leaves, tap the corner of the flat brush using paint left after stroking shading.
5. Highlight with light green (Lime Yellow + Lemonade. Use a #1 or #2 round brush flattened when loading with paint for this. See Fig. 12.
6. Paint center veins in leaves using a 10/0 liner and the highlight mixture thinned with water.
7. Paint side veins either light green (Lime Yellow + Lemonade) or darker green (Teal Green) depending on whether you're painting on light or dark areas of the leaf. Use the paint mixture that contrasts with the leaf color. See Worksheet, Fig. 13.
8. Paint veins on the bud using a liner brush with dark green (Teal Green) thinned with water. See Fig. 12.

Continued on next page

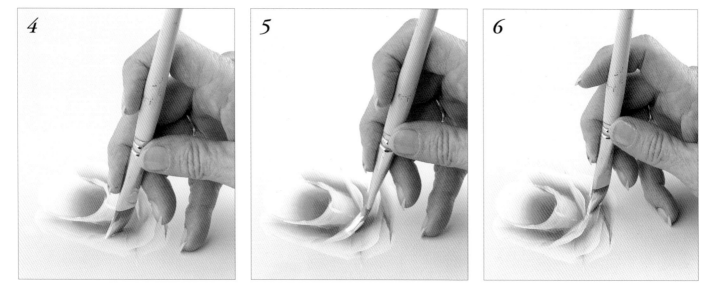

How to Paint Roses (cont.)

Finish the rose hip:

1. Stroke calyx on rose hip with soft green (Gray Green). See Worksheet, Fig. 12.
2. Stroke shading on calyx (Teal Green + small amounts of Burnt Umber) using a small flat brush sideloaded with paint. See Fig. 13. Let dry.
3. Highlight with light green (Lime Yellow + Lemonade). See Fig. 13.
4. Add tints of reddish brown (Burnt Sienna + Burnt Umber). See Worksheet, Fig. 11.
5. Paint dried stamen using a liner brush and medium brown (Linen + small amounts of Burnt Sienna). See Worksheet, Fig. 11. Tap tips of bristles along the stamen to create splotches. See Fig. 12. Add a few yellow (Sunflower) highlights on the stamen using the tips of bristles of liner brush. See Fig. 13.

Finish stems:

1. Shade stems with dark brown (Burnt Sienna + Burnt Umber). See Rose Worksheet, Fig. 10.
2. Paint thorns using a liner brush with brown (Burnt Sienna + Linen). See Fig. 12. Let dry.
3. Highlight thorns and stems with light reddish brown (Burnt Sienna + Linen + tiny amounts of Titanium White). See Fig. 12.
4. Paint leaf stems using the 10/0 liner brush with medium dark green (Teal Green + very tiny amounts of Linen).
5. Highlight stems with light green (Lime Yellow + Lemonade). See Worksheet, Fig. 13. ❏

Regal Roses Writing Table

This table was purchased from a home accessories shop and was already stained and finished. With the addition of a black crackled finish and elegant roses it truly is one of a kind.

Its intended purpose was a side table. The size and height makes it suitable to be used as a writing table. The drawer is just perfect for holding pens and paper. With a mirror, it would grace a small foyer with style.

PROJECT SUPPLIES

Project Surface:
Wooden table with drawer

Paints, Mediums & Finishes:
Crackle medium
Black acrylic paint
Brush-on satin finish varnish
Aerosol matte acrylic sealer
plus acrylic paints for painting roses

Tools & Other Supplies:
1" white bristle brush, for applying crackle medium
1" or 1-1/2" flat brush, for applying top coat of paint and final varnish
plus brushes for painting roses

PROJECT INSTRUCTIONS

Prepare the Surface

To duplicate the appearance of my table, begin with a piece that is already stained and varnished. See the General Information section of this book for instructions.

1. Brush a coat of crackle medium over the table apron, and the drawer front. Brush less crackle medium where you will paint the design. Let dry overnight.
2. Brush a black top coat over the crackle medium, using a large flat brush and black acrylic paint. Avoid brushing repeatedly in one area – you can soften the crackle medium. Cracks will appear as the paint dries. Let dry thoroughly.
3. Mist crackled area with matte acrylic sealer. Let dry.
4. Trace and transfer the design, using white transfer paper.

Paint the Design

Paint the design, following the instructions for "How to Paint Roses" in this section. See the Roses Worksheet. Allow paint to dry thoroughly.

Finish the Project

1. Erase any visible pattern lines.
2. Brush on a protective finish of satin varnish. ❏

Pattern for Side of Table Apron

Enlarge patterns at 145% or size to fit project surface.

Pattern for Front of Table Apron

CABBAGE ROSES

Cabbage roses are quite simple, since only two basic strokes are involved. Both are made with a sideloaded flat brush. Petals on the sides and back of the rose are slightly curved upwards, while the front petals have a downward dip to the strokes. Both strokes are made with the lightest color in the brush creating the tips of the petals. With just a little practice, you'll be able to paint these very quickly.

Brushes for Painting Cabbage Roses

Flats – #14, #12, #10, #8   Liners – #1, 10/0
Deerfoot stippler – 1/4" *or* old worn-out #4 or #6 flats

Acrylic Paints for Cabbage Roses

Burnt Umber	Burnt Sienna	Lemonade	Lime Yellow	Linen	Peach Perfection

Raspberry Wine	Teal Green	Thicket	Titanium White	Warm White

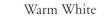

Landscape Worksheet

Fig. 1: Sky and water are painted; vines are basecoated.

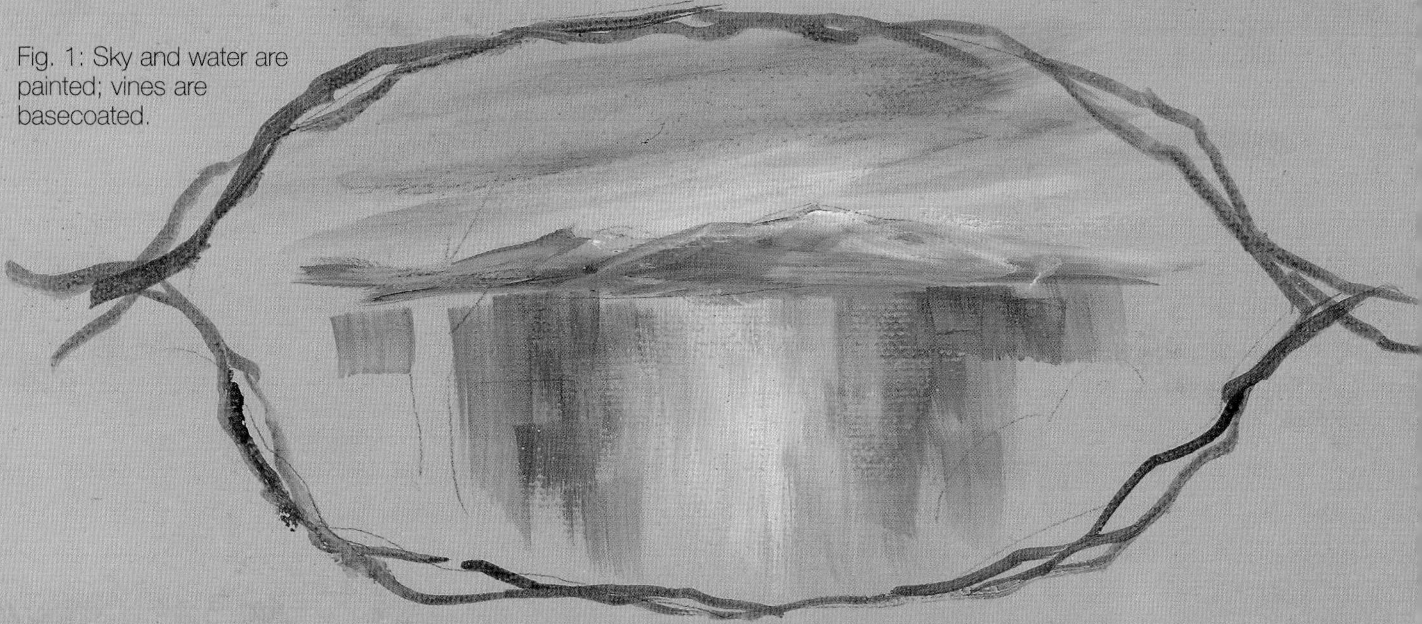

Fig. 2: Distant foliage is stippled.

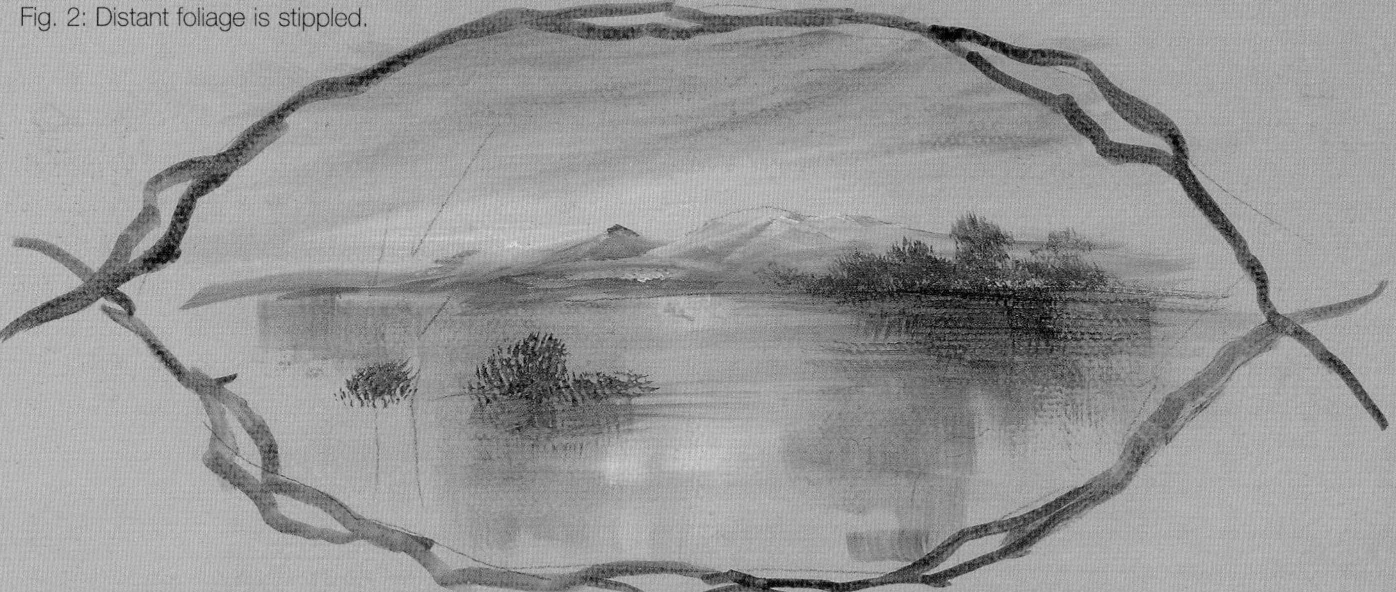

Fig. 3: Tree trunks and branches are added; near foliage is stippled; foliage is highlighted; vines are shaded and highlighted.

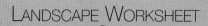

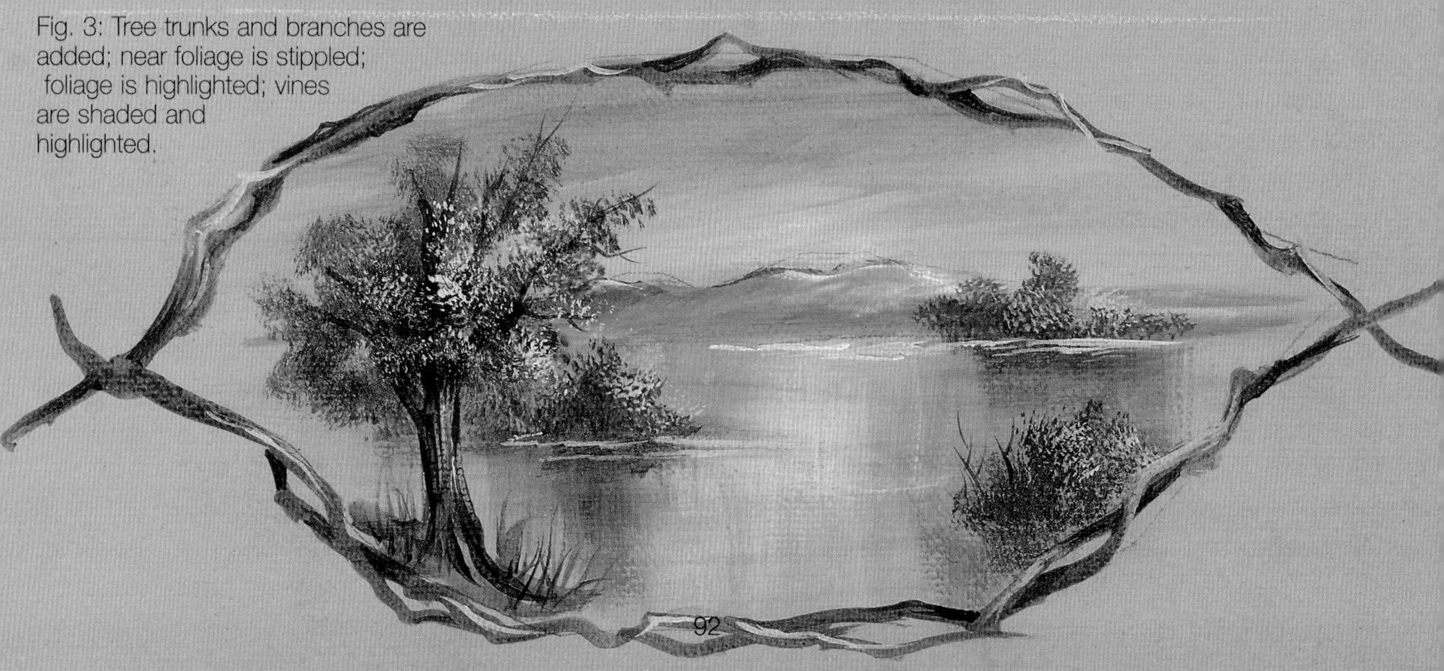

CABBAGE ROSES WORKSHEET

Fig. 1: Flower, branches, and leaves are basecoated.

Fig. 2: Back petals are added to the flower; shading on leaves is begun.

Fig. 3: Front petals are added; outside edges of the leaves are established.

Fig. 4: Final petals are added to the flower; branches are shaded and highlighted.

Fig. 5: Centers are added to flowers; transparent leaves and soft color are added around the design; splotches are added to leaves.

How to Paint Cabbage Roses

Basecoat:

One coat of paint is sufficient. See Cabbage Roses Worksheet, Fig. 1.

1. Basecoat leaves with beige (Linen), using small (#6 or #8) flat brushes.

2. Indicate roses with a circle of middle value pink (Peach Perfection).

3. Basecoat the branches using a liner with thinned dark brown (Burnt Umber).

Finish the roses:

Read these instructions before you begin and refer to the Cabbage Roses Worksheet.

1. Load a flat brush (#12 or #14) with pink (Peach Perfection) (**photo 1**. Brush second coat over the circle. While paint is still wet, sideload the dirty brush with dark red (Raspberry Wine) **photo 2**). Blend on palette (**photo 3**). Stroke shading in center and across bottom of rose (**photo 4**). See Worksheet, Fig. 1.

2. Sideload the dirty brush with ivory white (Warm White) (**photo 5**). Stroke brush on palette to blend (**photo 6**). Stroke back petal left petal (**photo** 7). Stroke back right petal (**photo 8**). Make center back stroke for petal **photo 9**). The light side of the brush is always on top, and the strokes are made with a upward curve. Two rows of petals complete this step (**photo 10**). See Worksheet, Fig. 2.

3. Reload the #12 or #14 flat brush with middle value pink (Peach Perfection). Sideload one side of the brush with dark red (Raspberry Wine *or* Raspberry Wine + small amounts of Burnt Sienna). Sideload the other side of brush with white (Titanium White). Stroke left front petal (**photo 11**). Begin in the center of the rose working outward. Starting where the first stroke ended and overlapping slightly, make a right front stroke (**photo 12**). These strokes are made with a downward curve. See the Worksheet, Fig. 3.

4. Continue making strokes to fill in the bottom of the rose, starting on the chisel edge of the brush on the left (**photo 13**). Pull to the flat side of the brush and lift (**photo 14**). For the petals on the right side, start at the center on the flat side of the brush and pull to the chisel edge (**photo 15**). Make one or two more strokes at the bottom (**photo 16**). For the final one or two petals, you may wish to switch to a smaller (#8 or #10) flat brush. See Worksheet, Fig. 4.

94

Finish the leaves:

1. Sideload a #8 or #10 flat brush with dark green (Teal Green). Shade next to the centers on one side and on the base (stem end) on the opposite side. See Worksheet, Fig. 2. Let dry.
2. Establish outside edges with the same brush sideloaded with dark green (Teal Green). See Worksheet, Fig. 3. On some leaves, use dark red (Raspberry Wine + small amounts of Burnt Sienna) to indicate leaf edges. To add splotches to leaves, tap the corner of the flat brush using paint left after stroking shading. See Fig. 5. Let dry.
3. Dry brush highlights on leaves. Use a #1 liner flattened when loading with light green (Lime Yellow + small amounts of Thicket + Titanium White). If the basecoat color is still visible in the highlight areas, additional highlights are necessary only on the most prominent leaves in the design. See Worksheet, Fig. 5.
4. Paint any visible stems to leaves using the 10/0 liner brush with thinned dark green (Teal Green).
5. Paint center veins in leaves and highlights on stems using light green (Lemonade + small amounts of Thicket + Titanium White). See Fig. 5.
6. Paint side veins with two values of green. On dark areas, use light green (Lemonade + small amounts of Thicket + Titanium White); on light areas of the leaf, use dark green (Teal Green thinned with water). See Fig. 5.

Finish the branches:

See the Cabbage Roses Worksheet, Fig. 4.

1. Brush on more dark brown (Burnt Umber) to shade them.
2. Highlight with a light brown mixture (white + small amounts of Burnt Sienna). Let dry.

Add details:

1. Add tiny dots of light yellow (Lemonade) in centers of roses using the tip of the 10/0 liner.
2. Stroke transparent leaf shapes at the outer edges of the design to make the arrangement appear fuller and more lush. Use a #10 or #12 flat brush and thinned green (Teal Green) or blue (Thunder Blue). For the softest appearance, moisten the surface prior to stroking leaves. ❑

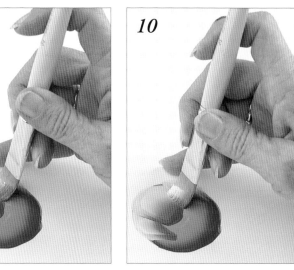

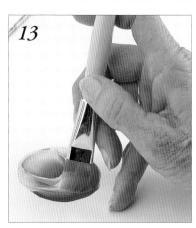
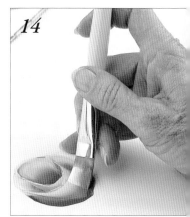

Console Table & Chair

*This narrow table was purchased unfinished at a local craft show. The chair came
from one of my favorite junk stores. They just seemed to fit together.
On the table apron, the cabbage roses are painted on either side of a landscape. I painted
sprays of roses, using the same colors and procedure as the table, on the front as well as
the back of the chair. By doing that, I could position the chair at the end of the table or
facing it and still have a coordinating design visible.*

PROJECT SUPPLIES

Project Surfaces:

Narrow wooden table with curved legs
  and apron

Wooden chair

Paints, Mediums & Finishes:

Aerosol stain-blocking sealer

Latex paint – Off-white

Acrylic paints – Soft pastel green
  (Gray Green), beige (Linen), ivory
  (Warm White)

Glazing medium – Metallic gold

Floating medium

Waterbase varnish

Acrylic paints for painting the
  landscape scene:

  Burnt Umber

  Burnt Sienna

  Lemonade

  Lime Yellow

  Raspberry Wine

  Raw Sienna

  Teal Green

  Thicket

  Thunder Blue

  Titanium White

plus acrylic paints for painting cabbage
  roses

Tools & Other Supplies:

1" sponge brush, for base painting

Painter's masking tape, for painting
  border

Clear ruler, for measuring border

Cosmetic sponge, for applying gold to
  edges of chair

Piece of natural sponge

plus brushes for painting cabbage roses

PROJECT INSTRUCTIONS

Prepare the Surface Background

Base paint:

1. Spray the table and chair with stain-blocking primer. (If they are white or light-colored, you can skip this step.)
2. Paint the tabletop with off-white. Paint the table apron and the legs with soft pastel green (Gray Green).
3. Paint the chair with soft pastel green. Two coats will be necessary for a smooth opaque coverage. Let paint dry and sand lightly between coats. Let dry completely.

Paint border:

1. Measure and mark placement of a border all around the tabletop. (Mine is 2" from outside edge and 1" wide.) Position tape on either side of the border, making sure the edges of the tape are secure on the surface.
2. Paint the border with Gray Green. A second coat may be necessary for a smooth, opaque coverage. Allow paint to dry. **Do not** remove tape.

Sponge:

*A sponged finish was added to the table legs and border and to the front and back of
the apron. Two colors thinned greatly with floating medium and water were used.
Allow the paint to dry between applications.*

1. Cut the sea sponge so you have a flat surface revealing a large irregular hole pattern.
2. Squeeze a small amount of beige (Linen) on a wax palette or paper plate. With a palette knife, mix floating medium and water with the paint to achieve a semi-transparent consistency. Wet the sponge with water and squeeze dry.
3. Dab sponge in paint mixture and rub sponge in a circular motion on the palette to distribute the paint. Apply by gently pressing the sponge to the surface. *Tip: The pattern will be more interesting if you press the flat side of the sponge to the surface rather than dabbing color on.*
4. Repeat these steps until all areas mentioned have been sponged. Allow to dry.
5. Add more sponging, this time with ivory (Warm White) that has been thinned greatly. See the General Information section for an example.
6. Remove tape from the border as soon as sponging is complete. Allow to dry thoroughly.

Continued on next page

Add gold trim:

1. Squeeze a small amount of gold glaze on a wax palette. Wet a cosmetic sponge with water and squeeze dry. Dab the sponge in the glaze and rub lightly in a circular motion on the palette to distribute the glaze in the sponge. Apply glaze to edges of the back panel of the chair. Use one continuous stroke of the sponge for a perfectly even edge.
2. Use a #20 flat brush to paint the grooved edges on the table sides. Let dry before handling.
3. Trace and transfer the design.

Paint the Scene

See the Landscape Worksheet.

Sky:

Paint the sky using paints thinned to a transparent consistency. It will be a bit easier if the surface is first moistened with small amounts of water + floating medium prior to stroking on paint. See the Landscape Worksheet, Fig. 1.

1. Using a large flat brush (#14 or #16), stroke thinned dark blue (Thunder Blue) across top of sky with a slightly downward motion.
2. While paint is still wet, stroke transparent dark red (Raspberry Wine) in middle area of sky.
3. Stroke tiny amounts of light yellow (Lemonade) next to the horizon. Blend lightly if necessary. Let dry.

Paint the water:

Use the large flat brush (#14 or 16) with paints thinned to a transparent consistency. Stroke paints on with a vertical stroke, wipe the brush, and blend lightly with horizontal strokes. Use the same colors as used in the sky. A surface slightly moistened with small amounts of water and floating medium will allow paints to stay blendable longer. See the Landscape Worksheet, Fig. 1.

1. Stroke on dark blue (Thunder Blue).
2. Stroke dark red (Raspberry Wine).
3. Stroke on light yellow (Lemonade). Wipe the brush and blend lightly in a horizontal fashion.

Paint the mountains:

Use a small (#8 or #10) flat brush and horizontal strokes. See the Landscape Worksheet, Fig. 2.

1. Brush a dark blue-purple (Thunder Blue + small amounts of Raspberry Wine) to indicate mountains.
2. Highlight with light blue (Thunder Blue + Titanium White). Let dry.

Stipple trees on far shore line and bushes on sides:

It is not necessary to moisten the surface prior to stippling the trees if attention has been given to the consistency of the paint. See the Landscape Worksheet, Fig. 2.

1. Thin medium green (Thicket) with water and floating medium and use a small deerfoot stippler or old worn-out flat brush to stipple the far trees.

2. Stipple some darker tree shapes using thinned dark green (Teal Green).

Paint the tree trunk and branches:

See the Landscape Worksheet, Fig. 3.

1. Paint the tree trunk using the #1 liner with thinned dark brown (Burnt Umber). Paint branches with the 10/0 liner and the same mixture.
2. Brush on more dark brown (Burnt Umber) to shade the trunk and branches.
3. Highlight with a light brown mixture (Titanium White + small amounts of Burnt Sienna). Let dry.

Stipple the tree foliage:

Use the 1/4" deerfoot stippler or an old, worn-out flat brush. See the Landscape Worksheet, Fig. 3.

1. Stipple all foliage areas with thinned medium green (Thicket).
2. Stipple darker (more dense) areas with thinned dark green (Teal Green or Teal Green + small amounts of Burnt Umber).
3. Stipple a few highlight areas of light green (Lime Yellow + small amounts of Thicket + Titanium White).

Add twining vines around the scene:

1. Thin dark brown (Burnt Umber) with water. Use the #1 liner to paint vines to enclose the scene. See Landscape Worksheet, Fig. 1. Let dry.
2. Stroke on more dark brown (Burnt Umber) to shade and light brown (Titanium White + small amounts of Burnt Sienna) to highlight. See Landscape Worksheet, Fig. 3.

Paint the Cabbage Roses

Paint the cabbage roses, following the instructions in the "How to Paint Cabbage Roses" section and referring to the Cabbage Roses Worksheet. Let dry.

Finish the Project

Enhance the painting with color added to the background:

Use minimal amounts of paint thinned with water and floating medium to a transparent consistency. See the Cabbage Roses Worksheet, Fig. 5.

1. Sideload the brush with paint and stroke color next to the main elements of the design. Colors appropriate to add to the background are dark green (Teal Green), dark red (Raspberry Wine) or dark blue (Thunder Blue).
2. Wipe the brush and blend with short overlapping strokes so the color gradually fades away. Let dry completely. *Tip: As I blend, I do not try to avoid surrounding leaves or flowers. After blending is complete, I wipe the background color off leaves or flowers with a clean damp brush.*

Varnish:

Protect the furniture with satin finish varnish. At least two coats are necessary for best protection. Let varnish dry between coats. ❏

Pattern for
Cabbage Roses
Chair Back

(actual size)

Pattern for
Cabbage Roses
Chair Apron

(actual size)

Pattern for Cabbage Roses Console Table
(actual size)

Connect pattern at dotted lines to complete.

SUNFLOWERS

Sunflowers are of the same botanical family as daisies and asters. Most have yellow petals and brown centers; some flowers can be as large as dinner plates. Many people grow them to attract pollinating birds and insects to the garden.

Acrylic Paints for Sunflowers

Aspen Green	Basil Green	Burnt Sienna	Burnt Umber	Lemonade	Pure Orange
Raw Sienna	Sunflower	Teal Green	Titanium White	Warm White	Yellow Ochre

How to Paint Sunflowers

Brushes for Painting Sunflowers

Flats – #12, #14, #16   Filberts – #8, #6, #4   Liner – 10/0   Filbert rake – 1/4"

Indicate main elements of the design:

See the Sunflower Worksheet, Fig. 1.

1. Paint the centers with reddish brown (Burnt Sienna), using a #6 or #8 filbert brush.
2. Use the same brush to paint flower petals with medium yellow (Sunflower). For separation where petals overlap, stroke a darker yellow (Sunflower + Yellow Ochre) while paint is still wet.
3. Paint leaves using a #14 or #16 flat brush with two colors to maintain contours. Brush on light green (Basil Green) in lightest areas of leaf and middle value green (Aspen Green) in remaining areas. Blend paints while still wet. Two coats may be necessary for a smooth opaque coverage. Let paint dry between applications.
4. Paint stems with light green (Basil Green).

Shade:

See the Sunflower Worksheet, Fig. 2.

1. Sideload a #14 or #16 flat brush with dark yellow (Raw Sienna + small amounts of Burnt Sienna) to stroke shading next to the center on back petals and the tips of the side and front petals.
2. Use #8 or 10 flat brush to stroke shading on sides of petals for separation.
3. Shade centers with the #14 or #16 flat brush and dark brown (Burnt Sienna + Burnt Umber).
4. Shade leaves with a large flat brush sideloaded with dark green (Teal Green). Stroke shading across back side (stem end) of leaf and down one side of the center. After paint is dry, a second application of the shading color can be applied, if necessary.

Add tints to some leaves and petals:

See the Sunflower Worksheet, Fig. 3.

1. Add reddish brown tints on some leaves using a side-loaded large flat brush with Burnt Sienna.
2. Tap splotches on leaves, using the corner of the brush.
3. Stroke tints on petals, using a flat brush sideloaded with Raw Sienna. Brighter tints can be added with thinned orange (Pure Orange) paint.

Highlight the various elements of the design:

1. Dry brush highlights on petals using a 1/4" filbert rake with light yellow (Lemonade + small amounts of Warm White). For brighter highlights, use a lighter yellow (Lemonade + White). Highlight front petals by beginning the stroke slightly on top of the center. Highlight side and back petals near the center and tips of the petals. Use a #4 filbert or a liner flattened as you load it. See the Worksheet, Fig. 3.
2. Stipple highlights on centers with dark yellow (Raw Sienna + Yellow Ochre) using an old, worn-out flat brush. Stipple brighter highlights with light yellow (Sunflower + Lemonade). See Sunflower Worksheet, Fig. 4.
3. Brush highlights on leaves using the 1/4" filbert rake with a light green (Lemonade + Basil Green).
4. Highlight stems using the liner brush with light green (Lemonade + Basil Green).

Add finishing details:

1. Use the liner brush to separate the petals next to the center using a dark brown mixture (Burnt Sienna + Burnt Umber) thinned with a bit of water. See Fig. 3.
2. Paint stems to leaves with dark green (Teal Green). See Fig. 3.
3. Underpaint stems with white. Let dry. See Fig. 3.
4. Paint stalks with light green (Basil Green + Lemonade). See Fig. 4.
5. Shade stalks with dark green (Teal Green). See Fig. 4.
6. Highlight stalks with light green (Lemonade + Basil Green). See Fig. 4. ❏

Fig. 1: The main elements of the design are indicated.

Fig. 2: Leaves, flower petals, and flower centers are shaded.

Fig. 3: Edges of leaf are indicated; tints are stoked on leaf; petals are highlighted and separated; stems and stalks are added.

Fig. 4: The painting is complete – centers are highlighted and stippled.

Rustic Chair
Metal Watering Can
Metal Birdhouse

Even in homes that are decidedly contemporary, a rustic grouping such as this one would add charm and surprise when used as a seasonal decoration. Visualize it on the front porch near the door on a late summer or fall evening, with the glow of a lamp softly lighting the entryway.

I loved the old, worn finish of this chair (from an estate sale) and did not want to alter it. I already had these rusty tin accessories just waiting for a moment of inspiration. The finish on the chair and my rusty tin pieces seemed perfect for sunflowers.

PROJECT SUPPLIES

Project Surfaces:

Wooden chair

Metal watering can (this one had been made into a lamp)

Metal birdhouse

Paints, Mediums & Finishes:

Matte acrylic sealer

Satin varnish (for chair)

plus acrylic paints for painting sunflowers

Tools & Other Supplies:

Soap, water, and old brush to scrub chair

1" brush, for applying varnish

Optional: Pen with permanent brown ink, metal sunflower garden ornament, small nails, rusty wire

plus brushes for painting sunflowers

PROJECT INSTRUCTIONS

Prepare the Surface Backgrounds

This is a painter's dream – little, if any, preparation before getting to the "fun stuff" of decorating!

1. Use an old vegetable brush and soap and warm water to remove the dirt and grime from the chair. (I worked outside on the patio.) Rinse with water and allow to dry.
2. Spray the rusty metal pieces with a light protective coat of matte acrylic sealer. Allow to dry.
3. Trace and transfer the design(s).

Paint the Design

See "How to Paint Sunflowers" and the Sunflower Worksheet earlier in this section.

Add the Lettering

1. Paint lettering with thinned dark brown (Burnt Umber). Let dry.
2. Add accent lines as desired using a liner and dark brown (Burnt Umber) or a pen with permanent brown ink.

Finish the Projects

Chair:

1. Brush a protective finish of satin varnish on the chair. Let dry.
2. *Option:* Use small nails to attach the rusty tin sunflower. Secure the flower stem to the chair with rusty wire.

Birdhouse and lamp base:

To maintain the matte finish of the lamp base and birdhouse, apply a protective coating of matte acrylic sealer. Let dry. ❏

Patterns for
Rustic Chair Back

(actual size)

Refer to photo for
placement of design

Pattern for Metal Watering Can
(actual size)

Pattern for Metal Birdhouse
Enlarge to 140% for actual size

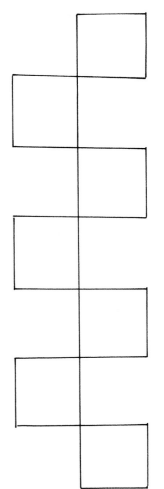

VIOLETS

When violets begin to peek from underneath their covering of fallen leaves in our woodlands and gardens it is a sure sign that Spring is on the way. Spring, a time of renewal and awakening, is my favorite season.

Brushes for Painting Violets

Flats – #14, #12, #10, #6, #4
Liners – #1, 10/0   Filberts – #4, #6   Filbert rake – 1/4"

Acrylic Paints for Violets

| Aspen Green | Dioxazine Purple | Lemonade | Night Sky |

| Periwinkle | Pure Orange | Teal Green | Titanium White |

VIOLETS WORKSHEET

Fig. 1: All elements of the design are indicated with paint.

Fig. 2: First shading is applied to leaves and petals.

Fig. 3: Shading is strengthened.

Fig. 4: Highlights are added to leaves and flowers; yellow tints are stroked on lower petals; the serrated edge is achieved on leaf edges.

How to Paint Violets

Establish all elements of the design:

See the Violets Worksheet, Fig. 1.

1. Paint leaves, stems, and calyxes with light green (Lemonade + small amounts of Aspen Green).
2. Stroke petals with light lavender (Titanium White + Periwinkle). Stroke smaller petals with the filbert brush and the lower petal with a flat brush. Let paint dry.

Create dimension within the design with the first application of shading:

See the Violets Worksheet, Fig. 2.

1. Sideload a large flat brush with medium green (Aspen Green) and stroke shading next to the center vein on one side and across the back on the opposite side of leaves. Let paint dry.
2. Reload the brush and stroke shading on the outside edges of leaves.
3. Use a small flat brush or a liner to shade stems and calyxes.
4. Sideload a #10 flat brush with lavender (Periwinkle) to shade inside the throat and tips of petals.

Fig. 5: The painting is complete – details are added to flower centers; veins are added to petals and leaves. The background is enhanced with added color.

Lighten front petal and deepen shading:

See the Violets Worksheet, Fig. 3.

1. Sideload the large flat brush with dark green (Teal Green) and stroke shading next to the center and back sides of leaves.
2. Use a small flat brush or a liner to deepen shading on stems and calyxes with dark green (Teal Green).
3. Brighten large lower petals with very light yellow (Titanium White + a speck of Lemonade). Sideload a flat brush (#10 or #12) with the mixture, position the brush with the paint side touching the very top side next to the throat of the flower, and stroke across the petal. Let dry.
4. Use the same brush sideloaded with small amounts of color to shade inside the throats and tips of petals. For variety within a grouping, use red-purple (Dioxazine Purple) on some and blue-purple (Night Sky) on others.

Refine painting:

See the Violets Worksheet, Fig. 4.

1. Establish outside edges of the leaves with a large flat brush sideloaded with dark green (Teal Green).
2. Using a 1/4" filbert rake with light green (Lemonade + tiny amounts of Aspen Green + Titanium White), stroke highlights on leaves.
3. For brighter highlights, let paint dry and stroke a second application of paint.
4. Use a liner to highlight stems and calyxes.
5. Flatten a liner when loading with paint and stroke highlights on flower petals as necessary. Use white tinted with a minute amount of the shading color for this.

Finish the painting with final detail:

See the Violets Worksheet, Fig. 5.

1. Using the 10/0 liner with light green thinned with water (Lemonade + tiny amounts of Aspen Green + Titanium White), paint veins in the centers of all leaves and side veins located in darker areas of leaves. Use dark green (Teal Green) thinned with water for veins in lighter areas.
2. Lightly tap light yellow (Lemonade) on each side petal next to the throat to indicate pollen.
3. Add a tiny dot of orange (Pure Orange) in the throat to represent the pistil.
4. Use thinned purple (Night Sky + Dioxazine Purple) with the 10/0 liner brush to sparingly add veins on the flower petals. ❑

Drop Leaf Table
Metal Basket & Candle Jar

This little drop-leaf table was stored in my attic. A stained finish made it look dated, and it no longer fit my decor. I added a fresh coat of paint, spent pleasurable time decorating it, and once again have an accessory I am proud to display.

The metal basket and lid for the candle jar were just the right size to use as accessories with embellishments of violets.

PROJECT SUPPLIES

Surfaces:
Drop leaf table
Metal basket
Candle jar with lid

Paints, Mediums & Finishes:
Flat white aerosol stain blocking sealer/primer
Waterbase varnish, for chair
Matte acrylic sealer spray, for basket and jar lid
plus acrylic paints for painting violets

Tools & Other Supplies:
Sandpaper – Fine and medium grits
Large flat (at least 1") soft bristle brush, for varnishing
Pen with white ink
plus brushes for painting violets

PROJECT INSTRUCTIONS

Prepare the Surface Background
This table had an existing stained finish.
Table:
1. Sand surface to even out the areas to be decorated and remove gloss. Wipe away dust.
2. Spray with an even coat of white stain-blocking sealer/primer. Let dry.
3. Sand again to smooth the surface for painting and reveal the stained finish underneath.
4. Trace and transfer the design.

Candle Jar:
1. Sprayed the lid with white primer/sealer. (I used this for the base paint.) Let dry.
2. Trace and transfer the design.

Metal Basket:
I found this basket in my stash. It was already painted with a color that suited the table and chair.
Trace and transfer the design.

Paint the Design
Paint the design on all three pieces, following the instructions in this section for "How to Paint Violets." Refer to the Violets Worksheet. Allow paint to dry thoroughly.

Finish the Project
Table:
Protect the table with several coats of brush-on varnish.

Metal Basket:
1. Use a pen with white ink to write "Violets" all around the top edge. Let dry.
2. Spray with matte acrylic sealer.

Lid:
Spray with matte acrylic sealer. ❏

112

Patterns for Violet Drop-Leaf Table

(actual size)

Use photo as a guide for placement.

FOR JAR LID & METAL BASKET:

Refer to photo and use these design
elements to create patterns.

Pattern for Daisy & Aster Mirror

(actual size)

See instructions on page 121.

Corners

Bottom of
Mirror

BOUQUETS & RIBBONS

Different flowers can be combined to create bouquets of blossoms, giving you more options for using motifs and colors. I combined daisies and asters to create a design for the piece in this section. Ribbons are pretty and add texture to the design as well as providing flow and movement. They are easily added to the bouquet designs you create.

Ribbons

Acrylic Paints for Ribbons

Warm White	Titanium White	Periwinkle	Teal Green

BOUQUETS & RIBBONS WORKSHEET

The Flower Bouquet

The worksheet provides general guidance for painting flower bouquets. The floral design illustrated here includes roses, daisies, and asters. For instructions for painting the individual flowers, see the sections on those flowers earlier in this book.

Fig. 1: A design with only the main elements transferred. Transferring too much of a design is as confusing as not transferring enough.

Fig. 2: Leaves have been basecoated. Daisy and aster centers are basecoated to establish the placement of those flowers.

Fig. 3: To avoid confusion when painting a design with overlapping elements, the element farthest back (a rose) is painted first.

Fig. 4: The leaves (which have flowers in front of them) are painted next. Highlights are omitted until the entire design has been painted.

Fig. 5: Thinned paint is splotched around the daisy and aster centers to add depth to the design.

Fig. 6: When the background color is dry, daisy and aster petals are transferred and painted. (They could be easily painted freehand.)

Fig. 7: Details such as brightest highlights, veins, and pollen in flower centers are added in the last group of steps. Additional colors can be added to the background. (Notice that the colors of the asters are repeated behind the leaves on the left side.)

The addition of transparent sprays of leaves and tendrils softens and enlarges the design.

Ribbon

Ribbons easily fill space and give flow and movement to a design. Use a flat brush that is as wide as you want the ribbon to be.

Fig. 8: The shape is transferred and the basecoat is begun by painting the parts of the ribbon that are overlapped by other parts.

Fig. 9: The ribbon is established with additional strokes. Notice how they overlap the strokes in Fig. 8.

Fig. 10: Shading stroked on the back sections.

Fig. 11: Less intense shading is brushed on the front sections of the bow. Highlights are added after shading is dry. A picot edge is added with zigzag strokes from a liner brush – notice how the color changes.

How to Paint Ribbons
Brushes for Painting Ribbons
Liner – 10/0
Flats – the width you want the ribbon to be, plus #10 or #12 for shading

Ribbons are pretty, add extra texture, and can serve useful purposes in a design:

- Paint them in colors that repeat the main or secondary colors of a design or in colors that complement the design.

- Paint the tails of a bow in graceful curves that reflect the shape of the object on which the design is painted.

- When ribbons are painted white, use shading mixtures from leaves or flowers in the design to create unity in the painting.

Basecoat:
See the Bouquets & Ribbons Worksheet, Figs. 8 & 9.
Load the brush fully with Warm White thinned with water to a semi-transparent consistency. Stroke one section of the ribbon at a time, and stroke back sections first. Reload the brush and repeat the process until all sections have been painted. Make thin strokes with the tips of the bristles.

Paint wider portions of the ribbon with more of the bristles touching the surface. Allow to dry.

Shade and blend:
See the Bouquets & Ribbons Worksheet, Figs. 10 and 11.
Sideload the #10 or #12 flat brush with a soft gray (Periwinkle + small amounts of Teal Green). Stroke on shading, stroking *across* the ribbon. Blend with the smaller flat brush used to paint the ribbon or with a small mop brush, stroking the *length* of the ribbon. Let dry.

Highlight:
See the Bouquets & Ribbons Worksheet, Fig. 11.
Brush highlights of thinned white (Titanium White), using a liner that is flattened when loaded with paint. Softer highlights are created by brushing paint on a slightly moistened surface. Brighter highlights are achieved by brushing paint on a dry surface.

Add a picot edge:
See the Bouquets & Ribbons Worksheet, Fig. 11.
A picot edge can be created for more interest by painting a zigzag stroke on the edges of the bow. Note that the color of the zigzag stroke changes according to where it's painted. On light areas, use thinned white (Titanium White). On darker areas, use the shading mixture thinned to a light value.

Daisies & Asters Mirror

This beautiful mirror was a Dumpster find. Quite often I visit the Dumpster behind a local furniture store (with the store's permission) to retrieve discarded bubble wrap and strong boxes to use for packing and shipping my projects. On one such visit, my husband brought home two discarded cabinet doors. He removed the damaged center panels, replaced them with mirrors, and – voila! – more new surfaces to decorate. I chose to decorate this mirror frame with ribbons, daisies, and asters. It would be beautiful hanging over a low dresser or on a narrow wall in a bathroom or at the end of a hall.

PROJECT SUPPLIES

Project Surface:
Mirror with wooden frame

Paints, Mediums & Finishes:
White stain-blocking primer (brush-on kind)

Crackle medium

Acrylic paints – Metallic taupe, light blue gray (Dove Gray)

Waterbase varnish

plus acrylic paints to paint asters, daisies, and ribbons – see the lists in those sections

Tools & Other Supplies:
Small foam paint roller

1-1/2" sponge brush, for base painting

#20 flat brush, for applying crackle medium

plus brushes for painting asters, daisies, and ribbons – see the lists in those sections

PROJECT INSTRUCTIONS

Prepare the Surface Background

For more details, the General Instructions section.

1. Sand the finish to remove the gloss. Wipe away dust.
2. Brush stain-blocking primer on the flat surface only (leaving the rounded grooved areas unpainted – the stained finish will be the undercoat for the gilding to follow). Allow to dry.
3. Base paint the flat top surface with light blue grey (Dove Gray), using a small foam roller. Two coats were necessary for a smooth, opaque coverage. Let dry and sand lightly between coats.
4. Apply crackle medium to the grooved edges. Allow to dry.
5. Brush over the crackle medium with metallic taupe paint. Cracks will form, revealing the white paint underneath. (This closely resembles gilding.) Allow to dry completely.
6. Trace and transfer the design.

Paint the Design

Paint the design, following the instructions for "How to Paint Asters" (in the Asters section) and "How to Paint Daisies" (in the Daisies section) earlier in this book. Let all paint dry completely.

Finish the Project

Protect the mirror frame with two coats waterbase varnish. Let dry between coats.
❏

Pattern for Bottom of Mirror

See page 115 for additional patterns.

BEES & BUTTERFLIES

Bees and butterflies can be added to most any floral design. You can also use one bee or butterfly (or more) in areas where there is no painted floral design to make the overall decoration custom-designed for a specific piece. Several butterflies are illustrated. All are suitable for inclusion with the floral designs in this book. Choose the ones you like best.

Brushes for Painting Bees

Liner – 10/0   Flat – #6, #8

Brushes for Painting Butterflies

Flats – #10, #8, #6   Liner – 10/0

Acrylic Paints for Bees

Pure Black   Burnt Umber   Yellow Ochre

Sunflower   Lemonade   White

Acrylic Paints for Butterflies

Black   Turner's Yellow or Yellow Ochre   Raw Sienna

Coastal Blue   Burnt Umber   White

How to Paint Bees

See the Bees Worksheet.

1. Paint bodies, heads, legs, and antennae with black, using a liner brush. See Fig. 1. Let dry.
2. Moisten a #6 or #8 flat brush with water and sideload with black. Paint wings. See Fig. 1. Let dry.
3. Use a liner brush to indicate the stripes on the body, tapping on color with the tips of the bristles to give the illusion of fuzz. Do not thin the paint for this, and use three colors to create dimension. The bottom third of each stripe is dark yellow (Yellow Ochre), the middle third is medium yellow (Sunflower), and the top third is light yellow (Lemonade). See Fig. 2. Let dry.
4. With the liner and thinned black, indicate veins on the wings. See the Bees Worksheet, Fig. 2.
5. Sideload the flat brush with Burnt Umber. Shade across the bottom of the body. See Fig. 3.
6. Tap highlights on stripes with Lemonade + white. See Fig. 4. ❏

How to Paint Butterflies

See the Butterflies Worksheet.

1. Using the liner with black, paint body, antennae, and legs, if shown. See Fig. 1. Let dry.
2. Moisten a flat brush (appropriate to the size area being painted) with water. Sideload with color and stroke wings. See Fig. 1. Let dry.
3. *Option:* Add more color to the wings. See Fig. 2. Let dry.
4. *Option:* Moisten a flat brush with water, sideload with a second color and stroke the color on wings next to the body. See Fig. 5. Let dry.
5. Shade the wings. See Figs. 3, 6, and 7. Let dry.
6. Add details to wings, using a liner brush. Paint veins and/or markings. See Figs. 4, 5, 6, and 7. ❏

Pictured below: A closeup view of the Pansy Headboard. See section on "Pansies" for instructions.

Bees & Butterflies Worksheet

Bees

Fig. 1: Body, legs, and antennae are painted; a sideloaded brush is used to indicate wings.

Fig. 2: Stripes are tapped on; veins are added to wings.

Fig. 3: The body is shaded.

Fig. 4: The stripes are highlighted.

Butterflies

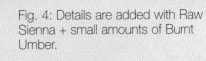

Fig. 1: Body and antennae are painted. (Legs are not visible.) Wings are stroked with pale color (white + a tiny bit of Yellow Ochre or Turner's Yellow).

Fig. 2: More color is added to the wings with a sideloaded brush (Yellow Ochre or Turner's Yellow).
Fig. 3: Wings are shaded (Raw Sienna).

Fig. 4: Details are added with Raw Sienna + small amounts of Burnt Umber.

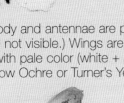

Fig. 5: Wings are stroked with two colors (Raw Sienna + Yellow Ochre on the edges, Coastal Blue next to the body).

Fig. 6: Wings are shaded, details are added with Raw Sienna + small amounts of Burnt Umber and Coastal Blue.

Fig. 7: A blue butterfly with blue details.

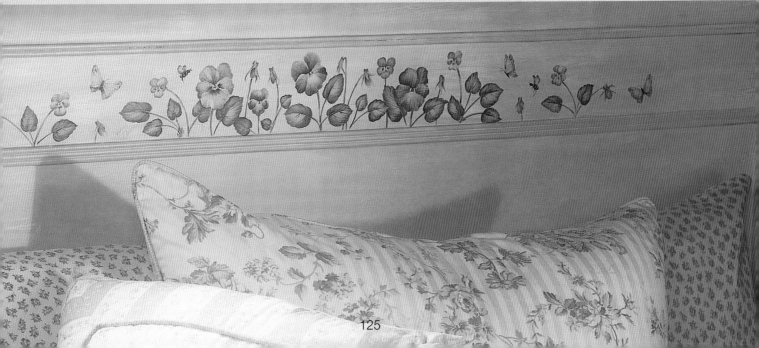

Pattern for Pansy Headboard

Enlarge at 130% or size to fit project surface.

A

A

B

Join pattern sections at dotted line to complete.

B

METRIC CONVERSION CHART
Inches to Millimeters and Centimeters

Inches	MM	CM		Yards	Meters
1/8	3	.3		1/8	.11
1/4	6	.6		1/4	.23
3/8	10	1.0		3/8	.34
1/2	13	1.3		1/2	.46
5/8	16	1.6		5/8	.57
3/4	19	1.9		3/4	.69
7/8	22	2.2		7/8	.80
1	25	2.5		1	.91
1-1/4	32	3.2		2	1.83
1-1/2	38	3.8		3	2.74
1-3/4	44	4.4		4	3.66
2	51	5.1		5	4.57
3	76	7.6		6	5.49
4	102	10.2		7	6.40
5	127	12.7		8	7.32
6	152	15.2		9	8.23
7	178	17.8		10	9.14
8	203	20.3			
9	229	22.9			
10	254	25.4			
11	279	27.9			
12	305	30.5			

INDEX